THE REAL
RYMAN
SETTER

THE REAL RYMAN SETTER

• A HISTORY with STORIES from the APPALACHIAN GROUSE COVERS •

Walter A. Lesser & Lisa M. Weisse

Foreword by Lefty Kreh

Schiffer Publishing Ltd®

4880 Lower Valley Road • Atglen, PA 19310

Copyright © 2013 by Walter A. Lesser and Lisa M. Weisse

Library of Congress Control Number: 2013948195

All rights reserved. No part of this work may be reproduced or used in any form or by any means—graphic, electronic, or mechanical, including photocopying or information storage and retrieval systems—without written permission from the publisher.

The scanning, uploading, and distribution of this book or any part thereof via the Internet or via any other means without the permission of the publisher is illegal and punishable by law. Please purchase only authorized editions and do not participate in or encourage the electronic piracy of copyrighted materials.
"Schiffer," "Schiffer Publishing, Ltd. & Design," and the "Design of pen and inkwell" are registered trademarks of Schiffer Publishing, Ltd.

Designed by Danielle D. Farmer
Cover Design by Justin Watkinson
Type set in Bookman Old Style/Akzidenz Grotesk CE Light
Photos by Walter A. Lesser unless otherwise noted.

ISBN: 978-0-7643-4513-5
Printed in China

Published by Schiffer Publishing, Ltd.
4880 Lower Valley Road
Atglen, PA 19310
Phone: (610) 593-1777; Fax: (610) 593-2002
E-mail: Info@schifferbooks.com

For our complete selection of fine books on this and related subjects, please visit our website at www.schifferbooks.com. You may also write for a free catalog.

This book may be purchased from the publisher. Please try your bookstore first.

We are always looking for people to write books on new and related subjects. If you have an idea for a book, please contact us at proposals@schifferbooks.com

Schiffer Publishing's titles are available at special discounts for bulk purchases for sales promotions or premiums. Special editions, including personalized covers, corporate imprints, and excerpts can be created in large quantities for special needs. For more information, contact the publisher.

This book is dedicated to my wife, Eleanore, who stood by me, except when I was wrong, worked with the setters for many years, and was always willing to take on a sick pup, if needed. Ellie was quick to come up with problem solutions, setter assessments, or help when decisions had to be made. This was no small wonder, since she had worked with English setters long before we got together. This work is also dedicated to our children, Hunter and Donna, who were there when the kennel work had to be done or helped me work dogs in the field. They were an inspiration throughout the manuscript preparation.

—WALTER LESSER

Rymans Birdy Anne.

Contents

Foreword *Lefty Kreh*

This is a book about Ryman setters, a grouse-hunting machine surrounded by controversy, but loved by those who hunted behind them.

I began hunting when ten years old and quickly decided that going for birds was much more exciting than chasing other game. Living close to Chesapeake Bay, I thrived on duck hunting and sought waterfowl as far as James Bay, where, hunched down in a snow-swept blind, Cree Indians, using only their voices, lured geese to our mud and feathered decoys. Quail, even turkey was exciting, as were other wild birds. But gradually my interest in other birds dimmed and I became a grouse hunter.

Living within half-hour drive of Maryland's Blue Ridge Mountains, I walked-up a lot of grouse that never fell to my 20 gauge. In Michigan, Pennsylvania, West Virginia, Maine, Nova Scotia, and other places, we often hunted with dogs. Most were frustrating or troublesome and they often spoiled rather than enhanced a hunt.

Then, with a Maryland hunting buddy, Raleigh Boaze, we spent two days near Elkins, West Virginia, with Walt Lesser and his Ryman setters. After hunting just one day with Walt and his Rymans, I was amazed and stunned. Walt is a low-key, easy-going fellow who never yelled at his dogs and often used a soft, gentling voice to encourage them. It was obvious that they both loved Walt and hunting. On the drive home, I told Raleigh, "From now on I am only hunting grouse with Walt and his Rymans."

Walt Lesser has spent most of his life attempting to keep the Ryman line intact. A biologist by training, a gentle person, and the most avid grouse hunter I know, he has spent time and money breeding a pure line. His wife Ellie handled all the chores of caring for the dogs, when Walt was either off on business or away with his gun.

After decades of working with Rymans, he joined Lisa Weisse to write this book. She has attempted to document the breeding history of what many believe is the finest grouse-hunting dog ever.

Walt tells of his introduction to the Rymans when he met the strain through author George Bird Evans. This began Walt's challenge of maintaining a setter standard designed by George Ryman, constantly trying to keep the lineage intact.

There is a marvelous chapter on the controversial George Ryman, for whom the strain is named. There are many stories about the crusty old Ryman, both good and some even nasty. Ryman wrote that he "disposed" of any dog he felt unworthy.

The book points out that in the early 1900s, when Ryman was developing the breed, much of our country was in new-growth timber—ideal habitat for grouse. The advantage of working and training dogs with abundant grouse is not possible today.

Lisa Weisse does a commendable job of documenting, with text and old photos, the history of the Rymans. It must have involved an enormous amount of research, the results of which Ryman friends will find fascinating.

A number of chapters are devoted to Walt hunting with his friends wherever grouse lived. If you are a hunter, you'll enjoy the experiences. If you read them carefully you will note that the text is filled with interesting and innovative suggestions of how best to work your dogs—as well as bagging the finest upland game bird in North America.

At this writing, I am nearing 86 years of age. For many seasons the highlight of the year was hunting grouse with my good friends Raleigh and Walt and those marvelous Rymans. After a hard day of following them through the rugged West Virginia hills, we would relax to one of Ellie's dinners.

In my late seventies, we came back to the house one evening, showered, and had a great dinner. On the five-hour drive home, I told Raleigh that, with great regret, I would have to give up grouse hunting. The hills had become too steep and the days too long. I maintained that Walt was in better shape than his dogs and I could no longer keep up with him. But I treasure the memories of fishing with him and Raleigh and seeing those wonderful Rymans locked on-point, as we flushed fleeting feather bombs. Read this book and, if you love Rymans, you will have trouble putting it down.

Lefty Kreh with Alder Run Tara.

Acknowledgments

First and foremost, I am indebted to Lisa M. Weisse for her monumental untiring effort and hours spent researching the many vintage Ryman pedigrees and Ryman's breeding history, and her development of the disc of pedigrees available with this book. Her work leaves little doubt concerning the makeup of the Ryman setter and will be much appreciated by anyone interested in this fabulous line of English setter.

We offer sincere gratitude for the research assistance and, in some cases, photographs received from: Linda Olszewski, Production Manager, *Field Dog Stud Book*; Bernard J. Matthys, American Field Publishing Company; Andrea Strobl, WillieWalker English and Llewellin Setter Database; Stephen H. Bell; Ed Morgan; and Carl Sillman, Historian, English Setter Association of America.

We are most indebted to the late Richard (Dick) Fox, who gave us ready access to his exceptionally well-researched database of pedigrees that includes all American, Canadian, and British show champions from the breed. Dick's advice and wealth of knowledge about English setters were crucial to the accuracy of the Ryman pedigrees and history. Without his help, and the cooperative efforts of everyone else involved, this work could not have been accomplished.

Appreciation is expressed here to John Thayer and Peter Zurbuch (deceased) for their assistance in the acquisition of the Ryman pedigree collection. Ryman sales listings, invaluable to our research, were very generously provided by the late H. Burnell Davis, Edward J. Matter, and James A. Mirro. Ryan Frame graciously provided a DVD of his interview with Ellen Ryman Calkins; all of which were of distinct benefit to our research. Botanical information for the "Salad Bowl" story was obtained from Paul J. Harmon, Joe Rieffenberger, and Thomas J. Allen (deceased), all of the West Virginia Division of Natural Resources. Our thanks also go to Wilson Davis for the liquor store and Mole Hill stories and Gary Spiers for vintage material provided.

The authors deeply appreciate photographs provided by Lefty Kreh; Tom Huggler, Outdoor Images; LeJay Graffious, Administrator, Old Hemlock Foundation; Dr. Harold E. Young and Nancy J. Young; Sandra L. Layton, Edward J. Matter, Susan Saling, and Dr. Fred Hyde. Lefty Kreh additionally offered valuable assistance in obtaining a publisher. Special thanks are due to George King, author of the book *That's Ruff,* for his great stories and quotes we used.

Our heartfelt thanks are extended to Hunter Lesser for the initial editing work and to Cliff Weisse for his invaluable feedback, editing, and a day of research at the American Kennel Club library. Donna Burks and Donna Lesser quickly came to the rescue when my computer skills were lacking—my thanks and appreciation for their patience and encouragement.

Our thanks also go to all those devoted people who cooperatively worked over the many years to keep the old Ryman bloodlines intact.

Many un-named people, mostly grouse hunters, helped us greatly along this journey by simply offering words of encouragement and inspiration. Our thanks go to all these folks.

I had the good fortune to pursue grouse and woodcock with Ryman setters at an early age, thanks to others who, for many years, had sorted through various gun dogs before deciding that these setters were the best they could find for the job at hand. As a result, I gained first-hand knowledge of George Ryman—the man who developed the Ryman setter. With these mentors, I gunned over dogs that were bred by Ryman. From this knowledge and experience I, along with a few committed gunners, set out to breed the same type of setter. I did so for forty years.

In this book, we meet George Ryman—a real diamond in the rough, a perfectionist, and a man dedicated to the breeding of fine setters. Ryman sought an improved type of English setter gun dog. He demonstrated the fine points of his dogs by entering them in both field trials and shows. In Ryman's words, he bred dogs "that are fit to shoot over in the field on game," and "fit to look at or have about the home the balance of the year and be appreciated."

These pages also reveal the final outcome of the Ryman Kennels. I witnessed what was left of the Ryman Kennels when it came to West Virginia. Following the breakup of the kennels, after two years of operation, I acquired a collection of Ryman setter pedigrees. These revealing documents were mostly originals, with beautifully scrolled edges and George Ryman's bold signature. Most importantly, the pedigree collection contains Ryman breeding information from the late teens throughout Ryman's career, along with that of Carl and Ellen Ryman Calkins after his death.

I was further blessed when Lisa Weisse, co-owner of October Setters Kennels, Island Park, Idaho, offered to research the pedigree collection. Lisa has long been involved breeding Ryman setters and I couldn't think of anyone better qualified to analyze the data in these pedigrees. She inspired me to expand this book. Countless hours of research went into the chapters authored by Lisa—a monumental effort!

The pedigrees, along with Ryman's wordy sales lists, provided sufficient data for Lisa to assemble a chronology of Ryman's breeding program and a description of the type of setter he sought. To our knowledge, this is the most detailed history of the Ryman setter to be published.

Also introduced are Laverack and Llewellin—two men generally credited as the originators of the modern setter in the United Kingdom, with a brief biography of each. In *Roots of the Rymans*, Lisa shows the development of the Laverack and Llewellin setters after they reached America's shores, leading the reader to a historical account of Ryman's breeding program.

My goals for writing this book have evolved as old friendships were renewed and new ones made. I hoped to tell the Ryman story as revealed through years of working with these dogs and collecting Ryman memorabilia. I also wanted to recognize a small group of Appalachian grouse dog breeders—very dedicated gunners who are jointly responsible for keeping the old Ryman bloodlines alive and well. None of us could have done this job alone. These breeders and some of the more prominent setters are central characters in the tale.

We will also explore Appalachian grouse hunting, starring the Ryman setters. These chapters examine handling and suggestions for hunting these dogs on grouse, along with unusual traits of the bird. Readers will also find some entertaining and humorous stories snatched right out of the Appalachian grouse thickets.

We have aimed to unlock the mystery of George Ryman and his setters. For the first time, questions have been answered that have puzzled gun dog aficionados for many years.

If these pages spark new interest and appreciation for these magnificent setters and their noble feathered quarry—we will have met our goal.

Walt Lesser
Elkins, West Virginia

PART 1
MEETING THE RYMAN SETTERS

Grouse and woodcock dogs are not for every man. I've never been able to separate the composite aroma of a favorite shooting coat and determine whether it is blood and feathers, gun oil, or dog drool that makes it smell so good. Upland shooting is like that, its elements are inseparable. But, if one is more essential, for me it is the dogs.

—George Bird Evans,
The Upland Shooting Life

George and Kay Evans with Ryman's Blue Heather and
Old Hemlock Jeb, 1958

Searching for the Perfect Bird Dog

I had been around dogs all my life, but, to me, hunting dogs meant Beagles...wonderful dogs at home or in the field. Hunting in New York State, I used beagles for rabbits and ring-necks. After working in West Virginia for a couple years, I decided it was about time to get a bird dog and seriously pursue grouse hunting in the rugged Appalachian hill country. Reviewing the traits of various pointing breeds made me think of owning a German Short-haired pointer. After all, I thought, I needed a close working dog to thoroughly work the thick covers I knew.

While employed as a wildlife biologist for the State of West Virginia, I was asked to fill in as an instructor of wildlife management courses at West Virginia University School of Forestry, since their sole wildlife professor moved on to bigger and better things. I accepted the offer and put my search for the "perfect" bird dog on hold.

Looking for an apartment to rent for the semester, I was met at the door of one such prospect by, of all things ... an English setter. An orange Belton setter to be exact, truly a magnificent looking dog, but sadly, she was deaf. The lady of the house assured me that she would introduce me to the breeder...a man and wife who lived at Brandonville, West Virginia, less than an hour's drive from where we stood. That couple was George Bird and Kay Evans. My gracious landlady arranged for me to meet George and Kay. We listened to George play a classical guitar and he interviewed me as a setter pup prospective owner. At the time, George had a fine litter of pups out of Ryman's Blue Heather sired by his Old Hemlock Ruff. A photo of Heather and her pups can be seen in *Troubles with Bird Dogs* by George Bird Evans. An even better photo of Heather is shown in *The Upland Shooting Life,* where Dixie, as a pup, is identified with her brothers. The pups in this litter were given Civil War period names and I was fortunate to be presented with Old Hemlock Jeb. Everything was falling in place for me.

Ryman's Blue Heather was a gorgeous blue Belton, true to the type in every way, but unfortunately ruined as a gun dog. She was a serious blinker; that is, she would hunt beautifully but clearly avoid birds, working up to a bird in high style and carefully circling around so as not to flush the bird. Upon weaning the pups, George had no further need for Heather and offered her to me. He thought perhaps she could eventually overcome her fear of birds, recognizing, of course, that this was a fault probably resulting from poor handling by a previous owner. George and I took Heather out for a workout; she would not leave George's side, as he would wave a handkerchief in the air over the dog in an attempt to get her to range. Heather bonded to me very well and lived with the family inside our home. I worked her on many wild and planted birds and she hunted beautifully...simply gliding through the covers but—other than an occasional flash point—continued to blink birds. I had thought of Heather as the ideal Ryman type setter—being short-coupled in body and of perfect head and body conformation, with a weight of 55 pounds.

I continued to work Heather, but her main purpose in life was to be a brood bitch.

She never did take to the kennel life, yet was a perfect house pet for a young family. Our children certainly treated her with kindness and could do most anything to Heather without annoying her. She would simply lie perfectly still and allow the kids to enjoy her. There was the occasion when our son, Hunter, placed several aluminum coasters on the flat of Heather's head before my wife or I knew what was going on. When we saw her, Heather was just lying as still as she could be with a very neat pile of coasters on her head, allowing Hunter to continue adding to the pile!

I was living in West Union, West Virginia, on Middle Island Creek (said to be the longest creek in the world). This part of the state was undergoing farm abandonment during the 1950s and natural succession was rapidly changing quail habitat to better suit ruffed grouse. By traveling along Middle Island Creek, between West Union and Middlebourne, I worked the recently abandoned farms and usually found at least one covey of quail at each location, with a few grouse found between the old farms. It was a wonderful opportunity to train dogs on wild birds. Unfortunately, one long hard winter shortly after nearly eliminated the quail! Grouse habitat continued to improve, but the quail never did bounce back to their once-abundant numbers.

George and Kay Evans worked their dogs on young pheasants in southern Pennsylvania during late summer and early fall. My wife, Ellie, and I accompanied them on one such excursion with Jeb and Heather, where I found out how well-suited, young pheasants were for working dogs, as they hold much better than adult ringnecks.

Early that same fall of 1958, I was introduced to West Virginia's Canaan Valley by Doy Rollyson, a state trapper who was checking on beaver damage complaints. Acre upon acre of alders greeted us, broken by aspen clones in this secluded, high-elevation valley, and it made me think only of woodcock. I had hunted woodcock with my beagles on Long Island, New York, as a boy. The covers there were small, nothing like I was now seeing in Canaan Valley. After checking with the owner of a large parcel in this enticing place, I made arrangements with George and Kay Evans to meet me at the Worden's Hotel in Davis. We then proceeded to Canaan Valley and experienced a great woodcock hunt, introducing 9-month old Dixie and Jeb to these wonderful birds and shooting over George's Ruff, Shadows, and Feathers.

George later named this cover "The Gates." He described the details of this very hunt in his books, *The Upland Shooting Life* and *Grouse & Woodcock in the Blackwater/Canaan*. George was enchanted with Canaan Valley and its woodcock, and frequented *The Gates* each year for at least thirty years of his gunning career.

George Bird Evans had given me a start with English setters and their training—but most especially, without full realization, he started me with a setter bred by George Ryman. Little did I know that Ryman's Blue Heather was to be the beginning of my line of Alder Run Ryman setters.

Ryman's Blue Heather with a litter sired by Old Hemlock Ruff.
Photo by Kay Evans, Courtesy of Kathryn H. Evans / Old Hemlock Foundation

Old Hemlock Jeb and Jubal at 6 weeks.
Photo by Kay Evans, Courtesy of Kathryn H. Evans / Old Hemlock Foundation

H. Burnell Davis with setters bred by George Ryman. Setters of the day (1950s) were not always stylish on point.

Mentors— Taken Under Wing

Being deeply involved with English setters and having access to abundant wild birds throughout West Virginia's Doddridge and Tyler Counties, I was looking for others with similar interests. As far as I could tell, there wasn't another bird dog or serious hunter of birds in or around West Union. I did have friends in other parts of the state that came in to hunt with me and enjoy the dogs. There was Ray Speaker, previously a scout for the Pittsburgh Pirates, and John Casto, son of "Pop" Casto, sporting goods store owner, gunsmith, and excellent taxidermist. There was my good friend Fred Willis, who was always ready for a hunt, and George Hanson, a fisheries biologist who had championship 'coon hounds and not only knew bird hunting but would hunt 'coons all night and birds the next day.

I had heard about a very active bird dog club in Parkersburg, in the Ohio River Valley, which conducted field trials sanctioned by the *American Field.* I spent many hours talking with two members of this club, who tried their darndest to get me and my setters involved in field trials. For a while, I was torn between an interest in field trials and working and hunting setters on wild birds. Although I enjoyed talking to the field trialers about dogs and reviewing pedigrees, I kept reminding myself that my original interest in running setters was for hunting wild birds in their natural habitat.

Then I met two wonderful people with Ryman setters, H. Burnell Davis and R. E. "Bud" Evans, both living in Pennsboro, a town twenty miles west of my home. Both men had hunted with bird dogs since age 9 or 10, and I remembered hearing them say, "we never had real good pointing dogs until we got the Ryman setters." That was good enough for me. It took them years to find the right dogs; why should I look any further? Burnell Davis owned and operated the Pennsboro Motel and lived next to the motel where his wife ran a beauty salon. He owned other properties, including the building that housed the state liquor store.

The liquor store was conveniently located just across the road from the motel—making it pretty handy when reserves were low. Actually, the only time I saw Burnell take a drink was after the grouse hunt, when he had me reach under the passenger seat to retrieve a bottle of the most inexpensive bourbon available—Cobbs Creek, as I recall. Under the seat also was a small vacuum bottle filled with the blackest coffee I had ever tasted. I remembered wondering which was used to chase which! I also remember forcing each of the drinks down, so as not to offend Burnell. With help to maintain the motel, Burnell was able to hunt grouse with his setters every day weather permitted, and that he did! He hunted well into his seventies, when his health started to decline. It was said Burnell once offered training services and guaranteed gun shyness cured or all fees returned. He loved to be in the gallery of the Parkersburg field trials and

I joined him on several occasions. We enjoyed comparing characteristics of different breeds in the running. We had a mutual friend in Dick Mitchell, a meat salesman turned trainer/ handler, who could recite from memory more pedigrees than I had seen at the time. I had an opportunity to watch, first hand, the difficulties in pursuing such a profession and the cost on one's health as a result.

Burnell's son, Wilson, was a banker in town and also operated the family farm, raising quality beef cattle. Recently, while talking with Wilson, I learned something about the old liquor store which the State of West Virginia had leased from the Davis family for a lot of years, but had been terminated. A group of Mormons had approached Wilson's wife, wanting to buy the building which previously housed the liquor store. Mrs. Davis told them "you can't make a church out of a liquor store"...after which the Mormons informed Mrs. Davis that they were fully capable of doing so, and they bought the building and did just that! When Wilson told me this story, he said, "you know, it should have but didn't create near the fuss that changing the name of the town 'Mole Hill' (a town just north of Pennsboro) to 'Mountain' did, when the Governor and all TV networks made such a to-do out of making a mountain out of a mole hill."

The more I learned about George Ryman's personality, the more I realized the similarities between Burnell and Ryman. Burnell was a no-nonsense person, appearing hard-nosed and gruff, yet sensitive at the right times. He had an interesting, very dry sense of humor and loved to tease me a lot.

While working dogs, the first thing I noticed was that Burnell rarely handled his dogs, or even spoke to them while they were in the cover. Whether we were just working dogs or grouse hunting over them, he would move along silently, letting the dogs do their thing with little-to-no interference on his part. Of course, silence was stressed if there was any indication of game from the dogs. Another thing became very obvious to me early on—it was not necessary for me to do what these mentors considered to be "overtraining." This is in reference to having these setters steady to wing and shot, in particular. The setters I saw would usually stop to flush naturally, and the handlers' thinking, regarding steadiness to wing, was that the dog needed to move out as soon as possible to recover a crippled bird. I was told, "these dogs knew more about grouse hunting than I did" and to let them think for themselves when it came to such things as how long to hold point and when to move on.

Burnell kept a pup from the breeding of Ryman's Sky Joe and Ryman's Blue Heather and named her Molly. Burnell started her in a Dolly Sods grouse cover at 7 months of age. Molly wasn't pointing at the time, but I'll never forget the smile on Burnell's face as she retrieved a grouse to his hand.

Molly developed into the kind of dog that could win a field trial, and I thought there was a spark of interest on Burnell's part to turn her over to a handler, but it just didn't happen. Molly had a good life with an aging grouse hunter during a decade with plentiful birds.

Like many of the old setters, Molly lost her hearing with age. She was killed by a car in Pennsboro. I had difficulty understanding this, since Burnell kept his dogs securely in a kennel building with attached runs and, living on U.S. Route 50, he was always very careful not to let a dog run loose. I discussed this with someone who knew Burnell and the dogs well, and it was suggested that he could have intentionally set Molly free, knowing she probably would be struck by a vehicle, and save him the pain of having her euthanized.

Bud and Burnell commonly shot cottontails over their setter's points—especially when they were close to their cars and didn't have to contend with the added

H. Burnell Davis with Alder Run Molly and a day's bag, after hunting with Walt in Canaan Valley, West Virginia.

weight in their game bags very long. The day I learned this, Burnell had taken a rabbit over one of the dog's points. He then opened his pocketknife and sharpened a couple branches on a young sassafras tree. He hung the rabbit head down on the sharpened ends of two branches, opened the body cavity and field dressed the bunny while the setter, who retrieved the rabbit, ate the entrails! I stood in amazement watching this act, and asked Burnell if he had tapeworm problems with his setters. He quickly whirled around and snapped the reply, "No! Why?" I realized that I had made my point by asking the question, but was surprised my mentor didn't seem to realize where these worms come from.

Burnell's final setter was purchased from Bob Sumner, whelped by Kathy's Devil Ann. Burnell's hunting had slowed considerably when he was in his mid- 70s. He was always a heavy smoker and passed away in 1982, one year after his wife, Nell, died. He consulted with me before placing his setter with Jim Rawson of Beverly, West Virginia.

R.E. "Bud" Evans was owner of a Coca Cola distribution plant also in Pennsboro and almost as avid a grouse and quail hunter as Burnell. Bud was a very generous person who genuinely believed in youth and did everything he could to help young people get a start in life, since he and his wife, Rae, had no children of their own—except, of course, for the dogs they had owned. Bud owned Ryman's Sky Joe who, crossed with Ryman's Blue Heather, was the start of my Alder Run Kennel.

Both Bud and Burnell had purchased dogs from George Ryman and related much information to me about the man who developed this outstanding strain of English setters. I had never met George Ryman. However, after discussing the man with various people who had—especially Bud and Burnell—I felt I knew him quite well. I collected all the information I could get my hands on relating to George and the Ryman setters. I happened on many of Ryman's early dog pedigrees, some catalogs and correspondence, talked to as many people as I could find interested in these setters, and looked at as many dogs as I could.

Prior to my arrival on the scene, Bud and Burnell had hunted together for 35 years and had been close partners in raising their setters. They accepted me well and took me under their wings as a youngster. Actually, they were enthralled with Ryman's Blue Heather, considering her Ryman-perfect conformation and also her color; she was a perfect blue Belton. Then something happened! I'm not sure what it was, but it involved some business matter. All I know is that Bud and Burnell never hunted together again. It was difficult for me to understand how these two men could be so close for so long and then become most bitter with each other, to the point neither wanted to talk about the matter. Although it made matters awkward for me, I maintained a close relationship with both men for the rest of their lives and hunted with them for as long as each would take to the hills.

I was very fortunate having both of these men show me the ways of grouse dogs and reasons why they had settled on the Ryman setters. They related why George Ryman bought several sons of the field trial champion, Sports Peerless, to improve the running ability of his strain of large, long-coupled, slower moving dogs. I had the opportunity to compare Bud's Ryman's Sky Joe—who had Sam Light's Skyrocket blood—to George Bird Evans' Old Hemlock dogs, who were slower moving, long-coupled, and larger dogs than the George Ryman type. The Old Hemlock setters, at that point in time, most resembled the classic show-type setter. I prefer the closer-coupled, smaller, and faster running dogs, with the great head conformation of the show setters—this to me is the Ryman setter type. I enjoy watching dogs run and the manner in which

R. E. "Bud" Evans with Ryman's Sky Joe.

they run, as well as the way they point. The former should be considered as a component of style, in my opinion. Pointing style was a matter of common discussion. The Ryman setter tail was expected to be held out straight or slightly raised over the axis of the dog's back. This is in contrast to the field trialer's "12 o'clock" tail—pointing skyward.

I recall one incident when Burnell's three setters had a bird pinned, all with tails pointing downward and in crouching or sitting positions. Burnell turned to me and said "Would you dispose of a dog for such poor style?" He asked this question proudly; knowing the dogs were rock solid on "their" bird—that was his primary concern.

Burnell used to say that he thought the best Ryman setters carried at least one-fourth field trial blood. My Alder Run setters were basically Ryman dogs, maintaining the early Ryman bloodlines by line breeding as long as we could do so, with a maximum of one-fourth field trial type lineage.

These two old bird hunters took this neophyte under wing and taught me much about bird hunting and training grouse dogs. They shared many hours of stories about what grouse, woodcock, and quail hunting was like in the West Virginia mountains during the 1930s. They also shared much about the history of this area, including the initial logging of the forest and the great numbers of grouse that resulted from this cutting and subsequent burning. It was their tradition to wait until after deer season in December before hunting grouse—even though the grouse season typically opened in mid-October.

Vegetation in the hill country of West Virginia was still too dense in October for serious grouse hunting, and many squirrel hunters (and, in later years, archery deer hunters) were in the woods at that time. Therefore, for the grouse season opening, these two hunters would travel east to "the mountains," the eastern, high elevation part of the state, where foliage conditions were usually two weeks more advanced and habitat conditions were more conducive to hunting. This region also was prime grouse habitat since being heavily cutover in the first two decades of the 1900s. My two mentors started hunting these mountains in the 1930s, which were likely the peak years of grouse numbers following the massive cutting and burning of the Appalachian woodlands.

Both men hunted with 12 gauge, Ithaca Model 37, "Featherlight" pump guns. After I came onto the scene, Burnell had his pump restocked with very fancy tiger-stripped sugar maple—both butt stock and forend.

Bud and Burnell joined me in Canaan Valley and surrounding mountains more than once during the month of October to work our setters on woodcock and grouse. There was one such hunt when the three of us drove to the top of Cabin Mountain to the Big Stonecoal Run and Breathed Mountain trailheads. We had let Bud off at the junction of the Cabin Mountain Trail to hunt alone with his setter Ryman's Sky Joe. Burnell and I hunted the Big Stonecoal Run drainage. We agreed to meet before dark at the Cabin Mountain trailhead where we left Bud and his setter. This being strange country to us at that time, we decided to stay along the trails until we were better acquainted with it. When Burnell and I arrived at the point we were to pick up Bud, neither he nor his setter were in sight! This gave us much cause for concern, as Bud was the oldest of this trio. I know we waited a long time for Bud to appear and, about the time we thought something had to be done besides waiting and worrying, a vehicle came up the road from Canaan Valley and stopped alongside of our vehicle. Bud, along with his setter, climbed out thanking the driver for the ride up the mountain and looking no worse for the wear. Bud got lost on Cabin Mountain and, instead of staying up high in the relatively

H. Burnell Davis after a successful Canaan Valley, West Virginia, hunt with (L. to R): Jeb, Maggie, Starr and Molly.

unbroken forest, wisely went downhill into Canaan Valley where he found the Freeland Run Road and obtained a ride to join us.

The Ryman setters owned by Bud and Burnell, and Ryman's Blue Heather, given to me by George Bird Evans, were quite a bit different from later "Rymans" that the Calkins' and DeCoverly Kennels were producing. The early setters were generally smaller, females averaging 45–50 lbs, with males running about 60–65 lbs. They were close-coupled, finer boned, and more athletic. I was shown that for grouse hunting I did not need a dog under my feet or a mechanically quartering dog, rather a dog that had the intelligence to know where to look for birds and go there in a smooth running style. Also, these setters adapted to the density of the cover they were hunting—ranging close in thick cover and wider in open cover, yet always keeping in touch with the handler. Sometimes, in very thick cover, the matter of checking in would simply be stopping and listening for the handler. For me, running dogs with bells was always desirable. When beeper collars came along, I used the "point signal only" mode in combination with the bell. The dogs learned to stop and listen for me without interference from the bell, a desirable form of checking in, as far as I was concerned. A simple unaided whistle, indicating my position, was all the dogs needed to continue the hunt. The more I saw of these dogs in the grouse woods, the more I was convinced these were the setters designed for such hunting. Much could be learned by spending all the time I could with Bud and Burnell while hunting grouse. I did just that!

My association with George Bird Evans was very helpful and inspirational, but unfortunately not long-lived by comparison. He invited me for a grouse hunt in one of his Preston County, West Virginia, home covers, as a return favor for our Canaan Valley woodcock hunt. I, in turn, had George join me on a Cheat Mountain grouse hunt, after which Ellie and I had dinner with George and Kay at the well-known Beverly restaurant, "Far Away Hills"—overlooking the country we had just hunted. I very much enjoyed the times we had together, getting to know their setters and visiting their beautiful, vintage Old Hemlock home. George mostly hunted alone while Kay took movies or photographs. I had the feeling they were not close to anyone.

The Worden's Hotel in Davis was a gathering place for bird hunters in October and November—a place where we could all sit down to dinner and discuss the day's hunt. It was the only hotel I knew with an inside kennel accessible from the outside for guests. George preferred to stay at a cabin at Blackwater Falls State Park, but would stop by the hotel and call from the front door to ask, "Are the birds being found high or low?" I don't remember him getting an answer. This was George's way, rather than sitting down at a table and joining in the conversation.

George expressed a desire to breed his Old Hemlock Briar to my orange Belton Tinker. I agreed to this proposal, although had some fear about the size difference between these dogs. I had not hunted with Briar but was confident he was a good grouse dog. Briar was a gorgeous setter, but very large. My Tinker, also a beautiful dog and very nicely conformed, weighed only 45-48 pounds. She was more like the Ryman type for bitches. Tinker was a great running dog and taught me to appreciate her size and athletic ability.

The matter of dog size, plus an intense desire to stay with the early Ryman bloodlines, led me to another orange Belton stud dog owned by Robert Sumner. It was Sumner's first setter, bred by George Hanson. Bob Sumner was working for Dave Francis, a farmer/coal operator who hired Sumner to manage a shooting preserve on Kathy's Farms, near Lewisburg, West Virginia. Bob, who I first knew as a fisheries technician for the West

George Bird Evans with Old Hemlock Ruff, 1958.

Worden's Hotel in Davis, West Virginia.

Virginia Division of Natural Resources (DNR) working under George Hanson at the Romney office, suggested that I borrow his stud dog and work him on grouse. The dog, Shadbush Ryman's Ruff, was a good looking, heavy-boned setter that worked birds well, much to my satisfaction. I knew this was the ideal mate for my Tinker.

Realizing I had a potential problem on my hands, I contacted George Evans and, in a full page and one half letter, explained my reasons for wanting to breed Tinker to Bob Sumner's Ruff instead of Old Hemlock Briar. By the reply I got, I knew I had done something akin to slapping George in the face! I certainly didn't want it to be that way. My decision was partly responsible for destroying an otherwise very friendly relationship.

I remembered George once making a statement, in reference to dog breeding, that he was "one step ahead of George Ryman" (Burnell had a lot of fun with this comment). It occurred to me that it had been a long time since George Ryman had used show bench setters in his breeding; he did so at a time when such setters excelled in the field on game as well as on the bench. Evans achieved his ideal type in Old Hemlock Ruff and, to retain the beauty he had in Ruff, he had purchased Wilda from the Blue Bar Kennels near Hanover, Pennsylvania. Wilda was strictly bench bred, with no field background. Evans was told that she was "birdy," and went on to say "I learned that they meant she pointed butterflies. She never quite got butterflies out of her mentality in her short and wild life." Wilda would not hunt for George—George had to hunt for her. Apparently, Wilda never pointed a grouse, yet she was bred to Ruff twice before two years of age! Obviously, breeding for her type and conformation was George's top priority.

After two large litters, Evans said, "They (the pups) had everything we could ask, with one exception: we had weakened the pointing instinct." I realized, then, that I was more impressed with the shorter coupled, smaller, and faster working Ryman dogs that I was seeing than the larger, long-coupled, and slower working Old Hemlock dogs. As a grouse dog breeder of sorts, I was committed to breeding only the best grouse dogs that a small group of us possessed. Overall conformation was next on my list of priorities. Looking back over the years, I had very few dogs that did not point or failed to meet grouse dog criteria. When I did, the dog was placed in a good home for use as a pet.

Many years ago, the grouse season in West Virginia was extended through the month of February. I remember telling George about the proposed lengthy season—his reaction was, "My God, I'll never get any work done." The state wildlife agency extended the season to afford more recreation time, as there was no scientific evidence that additional hunting would adversely effect grouse populations. Apparently, George thought he would be compelled to hunt every day of the season.

George had an ongoing battle with biologists and the West Virginia Division of Natural Resources (DNR) about the scarcity of grouse and the reasons for their low numbers. He discussed this in more than one of his books. Readers of these books soon see how George felt about wildlife biologists. I'm certain this matter affected our relationship as well!

Evans chose not to cooperate with a state program asking grouse hunters to submit wing and tailfeather samples, along with flushing rate data at the season's close. Biologists requested cooperators to record grouse flushes on an hourly basis. Various states record this data in the same manner. George Evans did not agree with this system; he recorded his data as the number of grouse per cover—believing he could actually determine the number of grouse each of his covers held. By doing so, he refused to believe the findings of scientific wildlife studies that grouse (and wild turkeys) move a lot more than was previously thought.

In George's 1994 publication, *Grouse on The Mountain,* he describes gunning along 34 miles of Chestnut Ridge between the years 1925 and 1967. In late October 1948, George started hunting the 13,000-acre Cooper's Rock State Forest in which timber had been exploited in the 1930s. This broad-scale cutting left the Forest in prime grouse habitat, and it was still producing good numbers of birds when George started gunning there.

Old Hemlock Setters: Shadows, Ruff, Feathers, and Dixie.

By 1958, when I began my wildlife habitat work at Cooper's Rock, the trees had grown into what foresters call a "pole-stage" forest or a "biological desert." The trees were too young for mast production, with an open park-like understory which lacks cover for birds and animals.

Throughout this book, George blamed the scarcity of grouse on over-gunning rather than the habitat changes that had taken place. The grouse and deer habitat was so poor when I started my work on this forest that one of my projects consisted of making ¼-acre clearcuts in grapevine areas to create islands of grapevine jungle—developing areas that provided both food and cover for wildlife.

In *Grouse & Woodcock in the Blackwater/ Canaan,* George revealed his feelings towards biologists and the West Virginia Division of Natural Resources:

> On October 22nd in 1958, Kay and I and our Old Hemlock setters gunned woodcock in the Canaan Valley for the first time. In those days I still had faith in game managers and the West Virginia DNR, and we had placed Dixie's brother Jeb with one of their biologists who wanted to show me a woodcock covert he had found in the Canaan.

Yet George paid me the best compliment he possibly could with the last paragraph of the same story:

> As we drove out with the fog gathering around us, I had no doubt that the Valley coverts were stiff with woodcock on that enchanted night, stopping in on their long flight south. I couldn't know what those aspens and those hawthorns and those alders where we hunted that day, which we came to call "The Gates," would mean to the Old Hemlock setters and Kay and me for more than thirty years.

I value the fellowship, hunts, and dog training we had together and felt that I was the one who gained from these experiences. I have enjoyed George's writings, as many also do, based on the collector-value of his books.

I felt extremely fortunate in knowing and working with these three men, considering the differences in their personalities and the dogs they had during the years we had together.

George Bird Evans with Old Hemlock Dixie in his lap and Old Hemlock Ruff.

PART II
GEORGE RYMAN AND HIS SETTERS

The dog knows what is grouseward better than you do. You will do well to follow him closely, reading from the cock of his ears the story the breeze is telling.

—Aldo Leopold,
A Sand County Almanac and Sketches Here and There

Chapter 3

George Ryman's Legacy

With their roots in early American Llewellins and the Mallwyd show dogs, the Ryman setters were a connection to breeding traditions of the past. Rymans were similar to the dual Llewellins of the late 1800s, yet, rather than being bred for competition, they were foot-hunting specialists with good looks from the show dogs. While numerous breeders of the early 1900s crossed show and field trial dogs, George Ryman was the most successful and famous breeder of this type of setter.

Ryman started breeding setters while living at Wilkes-Barre, Pennsylvania. There are Field Dog Stud Book records of Ryman-bred dogs being registered as early as 1913. He built his large kennels at Shohola Falls, Pennsylvania, in 1916. It has been said that he briefly had as many as 170 dogs, but had in the neighborhood of 50 dogs most of the time. He favored setters of the Laverack type, preferring fine-boned, square-muzzled, athletic dogs with Belton markings. He used dogs from the famous Sir Roger DeCoverly/ Sir Roger DeCoverly II bloodlines—renowned for setters that were fully capable in the grouse woods as well as on the show bench.

Early Ryman setter breedings were a blend of Llewellin field trial lines with that of the Laveracks, resulting in many being roughly half field trial and half show bred. Ryman proved his dogs mainly by hunting them on wild birds, but also by entering them in field trials and dog shows. For example, he had at least two field trial placements with Sir Roger de Coverly II, and won placements in the 1920 Westminster Show with three breeds—English and Gordon setter, and Pointer.

In the 1915 Pennsylvania Grouse-Dog Trial, Ryman tied for second place in the Shooting Dog Stake by handling his own Sir Roger De Coverly II, a blue Belton setter. Interestingly, in this same trial, Sir Roger II ran against his sire, Sir Roger De Coverly, "who had the reputation of being the best grouse dog in Eastern Pennsylvania, and the young dog out-birded his sire."[1] Show and field trial competition certainly helped Ryman achieve success in the establishment of his kennels.

This account is largely based on my collection of Ryman memorabilia. There is a collection of over 60 pedigrees and setter registrations salvaged when the Ryman Kennels were abandoned in West Virginia, along with several sales lists, stationery, a letter to Burnell Davis handwritten by Ryman, and various sales promotionals. Another key source of information was my close association with Burnell Davis who knew George Ryman. Davis, along with Bud Evans, had acquired dogs from Ryman and generously shared their knowledge and experience with me for many years.

Much has been published about George Ryman, but sadly a lot of it is speculative, inaccurate, or afflicted by personal bias. Other than the pedigrees, sales listings, and photographs, very little seems to have survived. Some of the pedigrees in my collection have an occasional note with a few words such as "this was a good one," but no more. Ryman's sales listings are informative with a skillful dose of salesmanship, usually with items of interest such as the dog's weight, conformation notes, and other characteristics. I learned much about Ryman from people like Burnell Davis, and reading the wordy sales lists that I have in the collection.

Show lines were prominent in the Ryman pedigrees throughout the 1930s, with Ryman owning dogs from the noted show breeding of Rummy Stagboro and Lakelands Nymph.[2] Later, there is evidence that Ryman became dissatisfied with the field performance of these Laveracks and placed less emphasis on show lines in his breeding program—even referring to the closely bred show dogs as "inbreds."

Ryman's crosses to Field Trial Hall of Fame, Sports Peerless, began in 1939. People familiar with the Ryman-type told me that this was due to his dogs becoming too large and slow. Burnell Davis described such dogs as being "lubberly," a word I did not believe was part of the English language! According to a Ryman sales list:

> I again saw I would soon need a new cross of setter blood. While I did not like to go back to the inbreds, I was more than fortunate to secure, by great luck, a fine son of Ch. Sports Peerless.[3]

The dog Ryman refers to was his popular Sport's Peerless High who delighted Ryman as a sire of quality pups.

Ryman wrote that he later purchased five more direct sons of Ch. Sports Peerless and one son of the National Champion Sports Peerless Pride. He describes the results:

> Much to my sorrow, it cost me thousands of dollars for the experiment. Son of National Champion won twelve first wins in field trials on his bird work, but as a sire he was just worthless: [Possibly talking about the dog 'Director'] so were three of the sons out of Ch. Sports Peerless. One son was fair and the other was a wobder [wonder?] but he produced many snippy heads, so there is no more honest proof in breeding anything than by experience. Many inquiries ask why I call them a Ryman-bred setter. My reply is because I bred them from costly experience as stated.

I recall hearing that of the Sports Peerless setters Ryman obtained, he selected one to further his breeding program and then disposed of the dog to keep others from using these same bloodlines. This might qualify as hearsay, however it has been recorded that he destroyed the sons of Sport's Peerless that he did not want to continue in his breeding program.

Ryman's Grouse Gladys was his favorite setter, according to Lee Stellrecht (personal communication), a friend of Ellen Ryman Calkins. Gladys was sired by Sport's Peerless High and out of Ryman's DeCoverly Glory. Ryman is quoted as saying in one of the sales listings that she was "the greatest bird finding handling setter I ever saw or owned in my life time."

In the Ryman pedigree collection there is a standard Field Dog Stud Book form showing the connection between George Ryman and the well known Grouse Ridge Kennels of Norwich, New York, founded and operated by Dr. T. M. Flanagan. In this unnamed pedigree, Dr. Flanagan had introduced the Ryman bloodlines through the sire's dam, who was Ryman's Grouse Marge out of Ellis's Royal Salute and Ryman's Grouse Gladys; again, Ryman's favorite setter. This might explain why the dogs in Grouse Ridge Kennels advertisements in the late 1950s to early 1960s resembled Ryman setters in conformation, thereby attracting our attention.

To carry the connection between George Ryman and Dr. Tom Flanagan a little further, in the 2010 Christmas Issue of *The American Field*, David A. Fletcher wrote "A Visit with Doctor Tom:"

> After establishing his urology practice in 1951, Tom went to Mr. George Ryman of Shohola [sic] Falls, Pa., for a setter hunting dog. The price: $400; she was named Ryman's Stylish

Thorn Lake Gary, a great looking stud dog Ryman bred to in 1937. Typical of the dogs Ryman used, Gary carried a mixed background of show and field lines. This is David Robertson, owner and operator of Thorn Lake Kennels, Lake Cary, Pennsylvania. *Photo courtesy of Dr. and Mrs. Harold E. Young, Jr. (relatives of David Meldrum Robertson)*

> Edna. Tom described her as a bulky Lavarack with lots of show blood in her veins, and she was truly a slow working "Gentleman's Gun Dog." Mr. Ryman advised him to pay him with two checks, one he could show his wife and the other one that could be kept out of sight.
>
> Ryman's Stylish Edna was the dog that started Dr. Flanagan on a "long and storied career as an amateur field trial competitor and breeder through his future enterprise, Grouse Ridge Kennels of fine setters, both hunting and field trial dogs."

Other well-known field trial setters appearing in the vintage pedigrees include such dogs as Nugym, a grandson of the 1911 National Champion, Eugene M; Sam L's Skyrocket; Chief Inspector; and Nugym's Rodney. All were grouse dogs.

Ryman grew up at the ideal time for a grouse hunter, with the original forests being cutover and the resulting young forest regeneration providing ideal habitat for grouse and woodcock. I doubt we will ever see such bird numbers again, because we will never see that degree of broad scale timber cutting. Early successional habitat (young forest growth) was widespread—the opposite extreme from present-day conditions.

Therefore, Ryman had no trouble finding birds for training purposes or shooting for the market, as he did in his younger years. With grouse and woodcock being so abundant during the early part of the 20th century, market conditions for bird dogs were also at their prime. Ryman's dogs quickly came to the attention of gunners looking for dogs that were easily trained and handled, and would produce birds for the gun stylishly and efficiently, while retaining the fine conformation of the Laverack setters. Ryman setters were very handsome dogs.

The 1920 article by Freeman Lloyd, following this chapter, gives us some idea of the type of wildlife habitat and bird numbers that surrounded the Ryman Kennels at that time.

The photographs of setters on stationery and in sales lists are very professional and I wondered if Ryman hired photographers. It has been written that Ryman did his own photography work, however I noticed a passage in one sales listing where Ryman requested prospective customers not to ask for photographs; "It takes a lot of time to even make pictures, as we are long distances to the photographer, but we do our best and its [sic] best to try to come direct to the kennels, and be your own judge."

Professional photographers may have been used in the early kennel years. During her 1999 interview with Ryan Frame (*Mrs. English Setter, Pointing Dog Journal,* May/June, 1999), Ellen Calkins said that George did his own photography, was "a wonderful photographer," and owned the best cameras.

Photographs in the various sales lists show the same dogs in very professional poses, just arranged differently on the pages, and are not at all connected to descriptions of dogs offered for sale. However, the dogs shown are very beautiful with good conformation—some with birds in their mouths.

The matter of Ryman having dog hides on display has been mentioned in the literature. George Bird Evans addressed this in his book *Introduces:*

> There was an outlandish tale that he had the skins of two of his favorite setters made into rugs in Ryman's office....and after being offered a beer [which Evans refused] while he was opening a bottle for himself I looked about, uncomfortable with the prospect of seeing one of the dog rugs, but I decided they must be in an inner sanctum reserved for more compatible guests.[4]

Burnell Davis told me that upon arriving at Ryman's office, in the early 1950s, he saw the hides of two setters hanging on the office wall, which Ryman described as examples of the perfect blue and orange Beltons.

There isn't much question about George Ryman being a crusty soul. He bred setters very selectively for the qualities he coveted and did not hide the fact that he culled individuals whenever necessary. He frequently referred to disposing of the "runt" in a litter, feeling the "runt" would never develop into the setter of his ideals. In Ryman's words:

> Even they said the runt made the best. Today I humanely destroy the runt. Poor breeding proves that the runt is almost like a midget in the human race....I made it my point in breeding to breed nothing but the best, level-headed dogs of each sex, fully trained and experienced on all birds. Of course, I killed off everything I thought would be small and a common setter. It took years of tiring experience at a large cost or expense.[3]

Such selective breeding certainly required heartless attention to the matter and was absolutely offensive to the majority. There is the story about an unsatisfied customer returning a dog to the Ryman kennels. After listening very carefully and asking questions, George Ryman went to his office and returned with a gun. He questioned the man once more and then shot the dog on the spot!

Ryman talked freely about his highly selective breeding. He gives us another bit of evidence along this line in his 1954 Fall Sales List:

> In my breeding, the first litter of a young bitch is raised and tested out on game. At six months old, many litters in my kennels have been completely destroyed if they did not rate up to my expectations. No breeder can tell what a new mating will produce in natural bird dogs in the field. That's a matter of experimenting. Why feed and breed culls?[5]

We found Ryman's writings in these sales lists to be of considerable help in understanding his breeding philosophy, his personality, and the very type of dog he was striving to produce. In the list presented about 1951, Ryman says:

> As I stated in my sales list back in the

> year 1935, that along, or in line with General recovery of business throughout AMERICA, my famous Gun Dog Kennels were enlarged in their breeding, rearing and training operations, for the better type of English setter, the DUAL TYPE: which means the kind that are fit to shoot over in the field on game, and the kind that are fit to look at or have about the home the balance of the year and be appreciated.

As result of the 1999 interview with Ellen Ryman Calkins, Ryan Frame published an article entitled "Mrs. English Setter," appearing in *Pointing Dog Journal,* May/June, 1999. During this interview, Ryman's widow explains much about the kennels, how the dogs were fed during the war years, and her active part in the kennel operation.

Ryan Frame gave me a DVD of this interview. I was particularly interested in any description Ellen Ryman gave of the dogs and the way Ryman handled them. She had explained that George imported dogs from England and that he would not breed a dog until it was proven on game. We could not find evidence in the pedigree examination of any Ryman-owned dogs imported from England. Every Ryman-owned imported dog found was from Canada. She talked about their tail style being "not too long" and when on point, being straight out or slightly above horizontal. Ellen said, "we liked short-coupled dogs"—much as I was led to believe from the setters I had or knew that Ryman had produced. Ellen said "patched puppies would be destroyed"— they wanted Beltons. I'm confident this philosophy changed over time, especially after introducing the Sports Peerless lines.

As a handler, Ellen described George as having "a loud penetrating voice that could make the dogs do what he wanted them to do." He exercised the dogs in winter by pulling a sled along the two miles of road to Milford (Route 6). There is a photograph in the sales lists of the dogs pulling a sled. George had a training camp in Canada (at a paper company camp), where he was able to lengthen his training season many months of the year. She described it as "a beautiful place," where there were "lots of grouse and good woodcock hunting." Ellen managed the kennels alone while George was in Canada. In the late 1940s, George spent more time on the Canadian training grounds and stayed there for longer periods of time. Ellen said, "George loved to be up there with the dogs and so many grouse and woodcock...I think he would rather be in Canada than at home."

Ryman was an excellent shot. George Bird Evans (*Introduces,* 1990) reported, "It was said he would lay a bet that he could walk up to a pointing dog with an empty gun, flush the grouse, load, and kill the bird." Ellen said of her husband: "George was an amazing wingshooter... I saw him flush two grouse in cover, shoot one, reload the gun and shoot the second."

There seems to be much confusion about George Ryman's setters in terms of size, athleticism, how they run, and so forth. Ryman had a particular setter in mind, a type, if you will, which he brought forth with his constant outcrossing. If we accomplish nothing else with this writing, we hope to get the point across that there were no Ryman setters produced after Ryman's death. Ryman's setters went through various stages of development following his death, especially concerning their size and conformation. We have found no evidence that the dogs were worked on grouse after Ryman's death.

Based on our research, even George Bird Evans did not appear to have a grasp on the Ryman type setter when he wrote: "The True Ryman setter is a big handsome lovable sort of laid-back fellow who can't be bothered with the nervous-gut attitude of field trial setters." Evans compared his Old Hemlock setters to Rymans by saying, "The Rymans have for years weighed considerably more than the

Old Hemlocks, have longer bodies and show less daylight under them. They are generally thought of as rather slow, close workers—an ideal of many grouse hunters—and in his letters to me, George Ryman spoke favorably of their 'trotting gate,' as opposed to the loping style of my setters."[4]

We believe Evans was describing setters being produced by the Calkins and that of DeCoverly Kennels—he couldn't be farther from the truth describing the type of setter George Ryman preferred and bred. This description certainly didn't fit Ryman's Blue Heather, who Evans bred to his Old Hemlock Ruff in 1958. Heather was a perfect example of a Ryman setter.

In our quest for evidence of just what the "true" Ryman setter was, we carefully examined several years of sales lists of setters Ryman was selling. We saw a predominance of setters in the 45 to 60 pound class along with descriptions and notes of their athletic ability. Ryman typically advertised his dogs as "The Perfect Gentleman's Shooting Dog" and "outstanding personal gun dogs with exceptional bird sense; close working, natural pointing, biddable...." thereby giving the impression he preferred slow, close-working dogs. We found abundant evidence to the contrary. There is little doubt that Ryman liked good moving, medium-sized, athletic dogs with exceptional bird locating and handling abilities. This is the type for which he bred.

Ryman's Birdy Anne, who is illustrated in the fall 1954 sales list, is a great example of the type of setter Ryman bred. Listed for sale in 1952, her photo was used in Ryman literature. She also appeared on the reverse side of stationary with the caption: "A Perfect Ryman Setter."

Birdy Anne's description in the 1952 sales list makes reference to the photograph of the "Perfect Ryman Setter." We are confident that this is Ryman's idea of a perfect setter in reference to size, weight, and conformation:

No. 9. **Birdy Anne**. Very light in color, white and orange ticked English setter bitch, medium size about 45 lbs in weight, she is a model in the setter type, has it all body head and tail, just five years old last August, steady hard worker, powerful nose, stylish as there be on point, note her style on point with gunner ready to flush the bird and make the kill. She is a grouse woodcock and pheasant dog, she is a direct Granddaughter of Sports Peerless on her sires side, on her Dams side she is all DeCoverly MacAllister and Imported blood lines of the old day bred setters just out of season. She is both house and car broken, have bred two good litters from her, a gun dog of the best and rarest blood lines left in setters. $550.

Ryman's Birdy Anne as she appeared on Ryman stationary.

To further the story of what Ryman considered to be the perfect setter, we contacted *American Field* and acquired a pedigree of Birdy Anne. It is our hope that this treatise on Ryman's Birdy Anne will give readers a more complete understanding of the setter type that Ryman preferred and strived for in his breeding program.

George Ryman suffered an incapacitating stroke in 1955, spelling the end of the George Ryman era. Ryman died in November 1961 at 72 years of age. The only public announcement of Ryman's death that I have found was a small obituary in *American Field* magazine.

Ellen Ryman continued the operation and management of the kennels through 1963. Ellen was no stranger to the dogs since she had been responsible for raising and evaluating pups and managed the kennels during Ryman's lengthy gunning trips in Canada. Ellen married Carl Calkins in 1963. Calkins was also very familiar with the Ryman setters, having owned them since 1931. Ellen and Carl Calkins successfully ran the kennels until 1975 when they sold the Ryman name and 70 remaining dogs to David Francis of Lewisburg, West Virginia.

Gravesite of George H. Ryman, Milford Cemetery, Milford, Pennsylvania. *Photo by Edward J. Matter*

PEDIGREE TREE

Peerless Seneca Boy

RYMAN'S BIRDY ANNE

Ryman's Grouse Trudy

Dolly is an example of excellent Ryman-type conformation in a modern setter.

Sport's Peerless	Iradell Sport
	Lady Burgess
Frandale's Veiled Lady	Bud's Jack O'Lantern
	Hillcrest Gypsy Queen
Duke of DeCoverly's	Roger DeCoverly Pete
	Queen of MacAllister
Ryman's Birdy Jean	Ryman's Woodcock Rock
	Canadian Nellie L

Chapter 3

The following article was taken from *Kennel News and Notes; Dogdom,* Sept. 1920, written by Freeman Lloyd. Mr. Lloyd was Kennel Editor of *Field and Stream* magazine. The authors thought this description of Ryman's kennel, dogs, "bungalow," and surrounding property to be very detailed and the only such information found for that point in time:

Paying my usual pleasant visit during the trouting season to George Ryman's splendid sporting estate at or near Shohola Falls. Pike County, Pennsylvania, it was, as usual, to find Rattlesnake Brook well stocked with speckled beauties, although it was rather hard to get at the pools because of the freshets from the heavy thunderstorms. A great country for the sportsman more than ordinarily fond of the hound, dog, gun and rod is this undulating, heavily wooded land, back of Lackawaxen and about thirteen miles from the station. As for the dogs, they are here aplenty, and right in a place where woodcock and grouse can be found at any moment within 200 yards of Mr. Ryman's bungalow, or as many would call it in other countries— shooting box. As I write this in the early morning at sun-up, and in his large front room or hall, it is to look out on a great expanse of bush and brush, with the lake that serves the Falls, glistening three miles away. Around the room are superbly stuffed birds and large game heads, and all set out on shields. English snipe, trout, and the picture of an all-white English setter dog are immediately over the writing desk, and glancing around the eye follows woodcock, ringnecked pheasant; a mink killing a partridge; ruffed grouse again, and yellow leg. These are all in groups and separated by superbly mounted deer heads, silver cups, guns, snowshoes and pictures of bird dogs; fishing rods in the corners and well away from the large open hearth. Here, indeed, is the sportsman's home with everything around, including bear, bobcat, deer skins for rugs, etc., etc. As for dogs, there must be a hundred adults, including English and straightbred Llewellin setters, pointers, griffons, German pointers and Chesapeake Bay dogs.

Among the setters there is a capital selection of Gordons, and it is pleasant to record that Mr. Ryman is now paying considerable attention to the handsome black and tans named for the Duke of Gordon and Richmond who established the variety. Imposing, sensible and steady dogs, they are just the ones for this heavy bushed and partridge holding Pike county, and for other places where such game localities are to be found. Every dog in these kennels is either thoroughly broken or is being handled every day of his life. Mr. Ryman has dogs and the game to break them on. Further, the accommodation and the kennels are very extensive, and situated in a bold and bracing situation, where the dogs exercise themselves in long and heavily foliaged runs, and take shelter in the raised kennels when they require it. Up at the end of the range is the dipping tank, and five or six minutes in this mixture made up by himself keeps Ryman's dogs as clean as smelts, and in capital coat. In these kennels, it must be explained, the large majority of the dogs are good and ready enough for bench show competition, and every one is the sportsman's dog—the sort he can shoot game over whilst he walks. In other words, they are not those streaks of lightning whose bird sense may be in their legs and tails; dogs that when they find game, a man has to *ride* up to 'em to make sure that he shall have a shot. Furthermore, the good looks and elegance in such dogs sometimes, if not often, are entirely wanting.

Examples of Ryman-bred setter conformation taken from the 1951 Ryman's Gun Dog Kennels sales list

Another example of Ryman bred setter conformation as taken from the 1951 Ryman's Gun Dog Kennels sales list

GROUSE DOG TRAINING

Fifteen years' experience in training the grouse dog has been my teacher. TRY ME and get an HONEST DEAL. Can handle a few derbys and all age dogs for the Middletown, N. Y., Connecticut and Pennsylvania Grouse trials. Will be on my training grounds after September 1st; my preserve of 15 thousand acres has an unlimited number of ruffed grouse and woodcock to train your dog on; pedigreed puppies and broken stock for sale at all times, the great grouse dog, a field trial and bench show winner, Sir Roger DeCoverly II, at stud at my kennels, fee $250. Write your wants.

RYMAN GUN DOG KENNELS Wilkes Barre, Pa.

Advertisement appearing in the September 1916 *Forest and Stream* magazine. Notice the address is Wilkes Barre, Pennsylvania, where Ryman started breeding his setters.

HIGH CLASS GUN DOGS

For Sale

The Great Wire-Haired Pointing Griffon bitch, Ophellia, registered, the winner bitch last year at the New York Show. She is true to type and coat; none better lives as a shooting bitch; a tireless hunter under perfect control; guaranteed in whelp to my stud dog Homers Georges Greylock; age, five years; price, $400 00. Her litter will more than pay for her as she is a great brooder; whelps eight and ten per litter.

Four high-class perfectly broken Irish setters; all registered; males, two to four years old; wonderfully well bred; stylish high-headed hunters, short straight tails, pep and style, all under perfect control, forced tender retrievers, dogs that hunt and find and handle birds, sold bank guaranteed or shown in the field here at my Training Kennels; all great stud dogs and good bench type; $400.00 to $500.00. If you want the best high-class dogs living, write me; otherwise, please do not reply.

RYMAN'S GUN DOG KENNELS, Shohola Falls, Pa.

Above & opposite page: Ryman advertisements from the April 1920 *Forest and Stream*, after the operation was moved to Shohola Falls.

ENGLISH, IRISH, GORDON SETTERS, GRIFFONS

AT STUD

The famous Laverack setter, **Ryman's Grouse Bobby**, a great bench winner and marvelous dog on grouse and woodcock; true to type and coat. Fee $35.

Superlative **Pure Llewellin Setter**, field-trial and bench show winner; a bird dog; actually the best Llewellin type in the country to-day. Fee $25.

Ryman's Grouse King. Part Laverack and Llewellin setter. One of the rarest, brainiest, bird-finding and trained dogs living. Fee $25.

Sir Rogèr de Coverley II, Jr. The chip off the old block; brains, bird-sense, type, coat, stamina, style; the snappy worker. Fee $25.

The Irish Setter, Ryman's Red Boy. Dark mahogany red; The greatest shooting dog of the breed—short, compact build, perfect head—short straight tail. Weight, 60 lbs. Fee $30. Breed to a shooting dog—with bench type—that is strong in producing natural bird dogs.

The Great Gordon Setter (imported from Scotland); true to type; wonderful broken dog. Fee $40.

The famous and broken **Wirehaired Pointing Griffon, Homer's George's Greylock.** True to coat and type; a bird dog barring none. Fee $50.

The Great Pointer, **Ryman's Fishel's Franknone.** None greater bred of that blood; true to type; wonderful bird-finder; an image of the late Fishel's Frank. Fee $25.

Every dog is one of my personal selections from experience. You get the value by breeding to them. All registered; perfectly broken and proven producers of great, natural bird-finding dogs with the old-fashioned true type. Enclose Postage for Stud Cards and Terms.

RYMAN'S GUNDOG KENNELS

SHOHOLA FALLS, PENNSYLVANIA

Guaranteed Gun Dogs For Sale

Wire Haired Pointing Griffon bitch four years old, true to type and color; excellent shooting bitch—no better; soon due in season. Reason for selling—she is same blood as my stud dog; price, $300.00. Three fine pointers; bench type; well bred, one a bench winner; two liver and white and ticked; one orange and white; very rare shooting dogs on Grouse, Woodcock and Quail; $175.00 each.

Three pure Blue Beltons with tan ticking, like paintings; bench type; three years old, real shooting dogs, registered, one a bench winner; all excellent stud dogs and fit to head any kennel; house and car broken; all tireless hunters; work to gun according to cover, $175.00 to $225.00. One of the best Gordon setters ever lived; staunch, steady, backs and retrieves; a real meat dog; very obedient; six years old; well bred, $200.00.

Two Blue Belton bitches, tan ticked, two and three years old, none beter in the field or in type or as brooders, $100.00 and $150.00. Fine liver and white and ticked female pointer broken on grouse and woodcock; registered; three years old; perfect bench type, $125.00. Every dog guaranteed as above stated; guaranteed good enough in type to win in almost the best of company on bench; all sound and healthy. These prices hold good till May 1st.

RYMAN'S GUNDOG KENNELS

SHOHOLA FALLS, PIKE CO., PA.

Fate of the Ryman Kennels

Robert E. Sumner was a young biology graduate working for District fisheries biologist George E. Hanson at Romney, West Virginia. Bob or "Bobbie" as George called him, hunted grouse with George and acquired an interest in the Ryman setters that would eventually steer him into another career. In the meantime, Bob was thinking about a career in fisheries biology and took advantage of further education supported by his employer, the State of West Virginia.

Upon graduation with a degree in fisheries science, Bob soon left his employment with the state and went to work for David L. Francis, a prominent farmer and coal operator near Lewisburg, West Virginia. Bob's assignment was to establish a shooting preserve on one of Francis' properties, called Kathy's Farms, situated north of Lewisburg along U.S. Route 219.

Bob was in need of gundogs and purchased a pup from George Hanson, which was named Shadbush Ryman's Ruff. Ruff was sired by Ryman's Mike Blue out of Alder Run Dawn. Dawn was a product of my very first litter of Ryman setters (Ryman's Sky Joe and Ryman's Blue Heather). Bob also purchased setters from Ellen and Carl Calkins for David Francis to serve their gunning needs on the shooting preserve and to establish a breeding program.

A brochure welcomed guests to "Kathy's Farm Fish & Game Club and Ryman's Gun Dog Kennels," and shows a log structure, the "Hunting Lodge: Located in old historic Greenbrier County nestled in West Virginia's Appalachian Mountains." This brochure lists David L. Francis as president with Bob Sumner as Operating V.P. The hunting preserve was a 335 acre section of Kathy's Farm located approximately 7 miles north of Lewisburg off Savannah Lane Road.

I visited with Bob on Kathy's Farm since he agreed to let me board Shadbush Ryman's Ruff while I tried him out in the grouse woods of Randolph County. If he worked out well on grouse, I had planned to breed him to my Seneca Grouse Tinker. Ruff was a large-boned, muscular orange Belton of true Ryman conformation and handled grouse, just as I expected he would. I bred him three times to Tinker with gratifying results. Alder Run Heather was a product of that breeding and was just about as perfect as they come. She was a wonderful companion of mine for 10½ years.

In 1975, Bob Sumner and David Francis bought what was left of the Ryman Kennels from Ellen and Carl Calkins. According to a letter by Carl Calkins, published in the Nov./Dec. 1991 issue of *Grouse Tales*; "We enjoyed these great dogs until 1975 when we sold the kennel and name to Mr. Francis of Kathy's Farm, Lewisburg, WV." Bob Sumner was mentioned in this letter as "Kennel Manager." Sumner and Francis purchased 70 setters and the right to use the Ryman name, officially relocating the kennels to the State of West Virginia. This negotiation followed the transfer of certain Ryman setters to Ken Alexander for furthering his breeding program under the name of DeCoverly.

In West Virginia, the kennels were moved from Kathy's Farm to a tract of land east of the town of Hillsboro and across the Greenbrier River. The only access to this tract was a ford of considerable length across the Greenbrier River, and a swinging footbridge.

This property was bordered on the east side by Watoga State Park.

Between 1975 and 1977, Bob Sumner operated the Ryman Kennels from the Hillsboro location on the picturesque Greenbrier River. During this time there was an effort to join forces with Ken Alexander in a joint breeding program. However, negotiations failed to materialize and, in 1977, each went separate ways. DeCoverly Kennels started with a large pool of Ryman bloodlines and Sumner's Ryman Kennels folded in bankruptcy.

I had visited Sumner's operation at the Hillsboro location to see the 70 dogs purchased from the Calkinses. I was most interested to examine his breeding stock. What I saw was extremely disappointing! There was at least one dog that looked more like a St. Bernard than an English setter—weighing no less than 125 lbs.! There were all sizes and colors, the latter ranging from almost jet black to snow white with few, if any, markings. There was no consistency in size, shape, or anything.

I was witnessing what I concluded to be the deterioration of the Ryman setter. It made me think that the Ryman blood existing in my own kennels, and that of a couple other "backyard breeders," was to be cherished and line bred as long as we possibly could. It made me wonder how long we could keep these vintage bloodlines intact without some outcross, as George Ryman did.

In the letter previously mentioned, Carl Calkins stated that "Bob Sumner introduced the small southern field trial type destroying the continuity of breeding and the Ryman type." By that statement, Carl Calkins blamed Sumner's out-crossing for the demise of the Ryman setter. To my knowledge, this was far from the truth.

I attributed the kennel's collapse to geographic isolation, poor breeding stock acquired from the Calkinses, and simple economics. I know the dogs had not been worked on grouse, perhaps for some years. It seemed to me that people had been taking advantage of the George Ryman name without selecting to breed the best grouse dogs. In fairness, the Calkinses were up in their years and perhaps not able to withstand the rigors of grouse hunting and Bob Sumner was handicapped by a polio affliction.

Following bankruptcy, the Hillsboro Ryman's kennel location was sold to two people who maintained the place with farm leases. They described finding the office with a leaking roof and the place in shambles. The early Ryman records, letters, etc., from Shohola Falls, Pennsylvania, were now water-soaked and ruined. Of two albums of old pedigrees found in the mess, only one could be salvaged. This album, containing 60 pedigrees and registrations dating from the early 1930s to the 1960s, is presently in my collection of Ryman memorabilia.

The fate of all the dogs is mostly left to conjecture. Those who had some contact with Bob said that he refused to talk about the dogs or anything connected to them. I did receive the following words from one of the new owners of this tract:

> When John and I bought the place there was 4 inches of water and a tremendous amount of trash on the floor. We hauled two truck loads of trash to the dump. John salvaged (I believe two record books) and gave you one…I did find the remains of an adult setter in one of the kennels. It was the mummified remains. I demolished all of the kennels and pushed all the boxes together and cremated the whole mess. The Kennel site is now back in meadow. I hope you can find the other book."

I contacted John who indicated they had only saved the single book which was given to me.

In the Calkinses' letter, both Carl and Ellen admit a falling out with Ken Alexander and the DeCoverly Kennels:

Since Ellen and I are along in years we have, and are passing all of the existing kennel records that we have over to Lee and Sheila Stellrecht, 6491 Pearl Street, Bliss, NY 14024. This includes photos, registrations, and pedigrees, original oil paintings and memorabilia. We leave them authorization to speak for us. Lee is a fine honest young man dedicated to reviving the Ryman Setter if at all possible. He is following George Ryman's precepts in an effort to reproduce the Ryman setter again. We wish him well and are helping in any way we can."

I thought it strange that the Calkins gave all this material to the Stellrechts rather than to Ken Alexander, even though George Bird Evans in 1990 (long after the Calkinses had retired) declared DeCoverly the Ryman line "heir." This reportedly angered the Calkinses.

My contacts with Lee Stellrecht led me to believe that neither Lee nor his wife, Sheila, were hunters, much less grouse hunters. Therefore, I had doubts that they were trying to continue their setters' interest in grouse. I had the distinct impression that they were simply "in love" with English setters, with no specific purpose in their breeding program. Lee reported to me that they had acquired *Pinewild* setters along with their Ryman dogs. The last I heard about the Stellrechts was that they separated as man and wife and are no longer breeding setters.

The Ryman name was used in *Field Dog Stud Book* (FDSB) registrations in the 1980s and early 1990s. In an email message dated April 08, 2003, Ken Alexander said "The Ryman name used after 1980 was by people using the name, often illegally or under false pretenses, to sell dogs." If the name was used illegally, as Ken Alexander stated, why would FDSB register these dogs using the Ryman name? The next bit of evidence concerning the Ryman name came to me in the September 11, 1993 issue of *The American Field.*

"RYMAN SETTER NOTICE"

I, Maurice H. Ryman, son of George H. Ryman, would like the interested sporting public to know that the "**Ryman**" name has been legally removed from the public domain.

The only authorized legal authority over the Ryman setter is myself, my wife Jean and John K. Fetters. As featured in April/May 1991 Gun Dog Magazine, the only source to authentic Ryman bloodlines is Ryman's Gun Dog Kennels, P.O. Box 89, Sandy Ridge, PA 16677.

Then, in the newsletter *Grouse Tales,* publisher Ken Szabo printed the following letter from Maurice H. Ryman entitled, "Ryman Gun Dog Kennel Controversy Ends!"

Dear Grouse Tales:
As of March 28, 1994, John K. Fetters of P.O. Box 89, Sandy Ridge, PA 16677, no longer has permission to use the name Ryman or Maurice H. Ryman in any form whatsoever. This includes his kennel name, signs, stationery, correspondence, etc.

I have consulted with Attorney Donald Young of Gilbert, PA about this matter. We both agree that Mr. Fetters has extremely overstepped his bounds...Copies of this notarized letter are being sent to the American Field, Grouse Tales, Gun Dog magazine, Pointing Dog Journal, And Raymond Gricai, Pennsylvania District Attorney."

Signed,
Maurice H. Ryman

The American Field Publishing Company has informed me that they have been accepting the Ryman name in *Field Dog Stud Book* registrations, but they will not issue a kennel to anyone with the name of Ryman Kennels.

CERTIFIED PEDIGREE

—ISSUED BY—

Ryman's Gun Dog Kennels

SHOHOLA FALLS, PIKE COUNTY, PA.

Name Ryman's Seneca Girl **Color** Blue Belton **Register No. F. D. S. B.**

Breed English Setter

Whelped April 10, 1946

Sex Female

Sire: Peerless Seneca Boy, F.D.S.B. 316818

- Sport's Peerless, F.D.S.B. 187632
  - Iredell Sport, F.D.S.B. 154714
    - Sport King
      - Petrea's Rex
        - Cherokee Marse Pat
        - Brownie Babe
      - Concord's Victoria R
        - Eugene Mead
        - Miss Beauty R
    - Alexanders Tiny
      - Mr Hart
        - Paliacho
        - Harts Babe Whitestone
      - Sloops Lady
        - Pine Croft Tony
        - Lady Flakes Leonard
  - Lady Burgess, F.D.S.B. 133693
    - Diamond Jack
      - Preachers Mack
        - Theodore Whitestone
        - Della Whitestone
      - Smiths Lady Louise
        - Caborrus Dock R
        - Speckle Mary
    - Bessie C Mohawk
      - Jake Mohawk
        - Joehawk
        - Jessie's Lady
      - Lady C Bell Linda
        - Commissioner
        - Bell-Linda
- Frandales' Veiled Lady, F.D.S.B. 265677
  - Bud's Jack O'Lantern, F.D.S.B. 135959
    - Eugene's Mr. Buddy
      - Mr Eugene M
        - Eugene M
        - Topsey Hawk
      - Speed's Momoney Beauty
        - Phillips Speed Ben
        - Momoney's Maud
    - Eugene's Miss Mickey
      - Mr Eugene's Supremus
        - Mr. Eugene M
        - Speed's Momoney Beau
      - Lottabrook Joe's Queen
        - Lottabrook Joe
        - Deuse's Ben's Bess
  - Hillcrest Gypsy Queen, F.D.S.B. 219395
    - Ponto Prince
      - Le Compte's Blue Ponto
        - Gore's Blue Pal
        - Le Compte's Queen
      - Clearview Queen
        - Clearview Don
        - Clearview Sue
    - Dennis Peggy
      - Pilot D
        - Mallwyd Monarch
        - Rackets Nell
      - Betty J
        - Whirlaway Spot
        - Roxan Rodfield

Dam: Ryman's Stylish Lady, F.D.S.B.

- Ch Mall'am Sonny Boy, A.K.C. 845090
  - Huntstone Blue Boy
    - Ch Gore's Blue Pal
      - Heather Shot Over
        - Leonidas of Ware
        - Ch Peg O'My Heart
      - Monte Carlo Topsy
        - Leonidas of Ware
        - Keatings Nellie
    - Le Compte's Queen
      - Simmons Count Jack
        - Island Count
        - Yadkin Diana
      - Jone's Trixie
        - Dock
        - Belle
  - Huntstone Rhoda
    - Ch Gore's Blue Pal
      - Heather Shot Over
        - Leonidas of Ware
        - Ch Peg O My Heart
      - Monte Carlo Topsy
        - Leonidas of Ware
        - Keatings Nellie
    - Huntstone Trudy
      - Bob of Cedar Hurst
        - Ch Britannia
        - Monomack Rhoda
      - Monomack Bess
        - Monomack Duke
        - Monomack Bell
- Patron's Lady MacAllister, A.K.C. A-175044
  - Pennine Patron, Eng. & American Bench winner Ch. Field Trial Winner in England
    - Mallwyd Roy
      - Beachley Haig
        - Glaisnock Jim
        - Craigielands Madge
      - Mallwyd Linda
        - Ch Mallwyd Albert
        - Kell View Nell
    - Misty of Coity
      - Marshfield Marksman
        - Rufflyn Clansman
        - Pentre Evelyn
      - Bryn Derlwyn Bess
        - Tynewydd Major
        - Coity Meg
  - Debonair Diana
    - Ch Albert's Mac Allister II
      - Alberts MacAllister
        - Ch Alberts Sir Alli
        - Alberts Grace
      - Superlative Jean
        - Superlative
        - Ryman's Miss Flo
    - O' D's Roxy
      - Foxboro Lemons
        - Ch Britannia
        - Jamaica Jacqueline
      - O'D's Freckles
        - Ch Britannia
        - Dainty Peggy

Breeder Geo. H. Ryman

Owner John R. Kernan.

The attached seal of Ryman's Gun Dog Kennels (Registered F. D. S. B. Vol. 17), Certifies that the above pedigree is compiled from the records of said Kennels.

Dated at Shohola Falls, Pike County, Pa., this 21st *day of* July 19 46

RYMAN'S GUN DOG KENNELS.

Geo. H. Ryman

PART III
RYMAN'S BREEDING HISTORY

• LISA M. WEISSE •

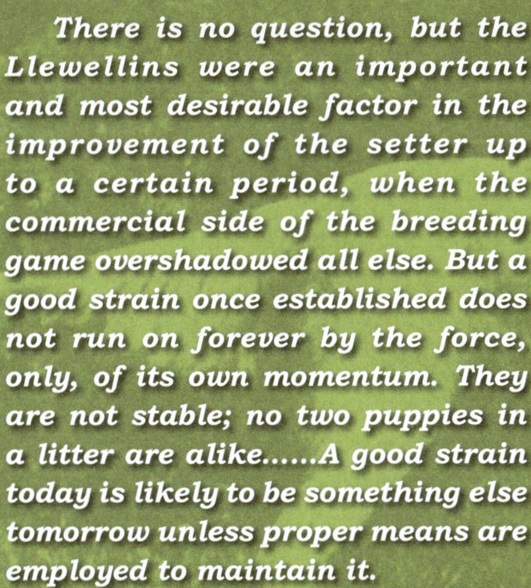

There is no question, but the Llewellins were an important and most desirable factor in the improvement of the setter up to a certain period, when the commercial side of the breeding game overshadowed all else. But a good strain once established does not run on forever by the force, only, of its own momentum. They are not stable; no two puppies in a litter are alike......A good strain today is likely to be something else tomorrow unless proper means are employed to maintain it.

—A. F. Hochwalt,
The Modern Setter, 1935 Edition.

Laverack and Llewellin
— Originators of the Modern Setter

To understand how the Ryman setters were developed it is important to first examine the formation of the English Setter in the United Kingdom. The history of the breed is a truly fascinating study and, as with the Rymans, the modern account of the early setters often does not match the historical records. From Llewellin stumbling into a lucky cross after being adrift as a breeder, to the idea that setters began as a homogenous breed of dual dogs, much of the "common knowledge" about the breed is myth and the records actually reveal a more intriguing story.

The setters of the British Isles are thought to have descended from the ancient Land or Setting Spaniel, references to which go back to the 15th century. These dogs were trained to help capture birds using nets and may have originally been used for falconry. Many early strains of setters were developed from them, often known for the region or estate where they were bred, or by their color. Eventually certain of the black and tan types became the Gordon Setters, named for the Duke of Gordon's kennel in Scotland. Irish Setters were reds, and the red and whites.

Among the various setters, the English was developed by a decidedly diverse array of breeders—distant from each other, and each with his own goals, personal standards, and "breed." No effort was conducted to mold this hereditary mass into a definite type and conformation until the advent of bench and field competition in the mid-1800s, when people began to pay attention to the setters of Edward Laverack.

Laverack

The story of the Laverack setters is a familiar one to most English Setter enthusiasts. In 1825, Edward Laverack acquired two setters called "Old Moll" and "Ponto" from Reverend A. Harrison, who had kept his strain pure for a period of 35 years, going back to 1790. Laverack bred this strain of setters for almost 50 years, during which time he claimed to have introduced no outside blood—all traced back exclusively to Old Moll and Ponto. The problem with this story is that it probably isn't true.

Writers of the era pointed out various reasons to doubt Laverack's pedigrees. They contained an impossibly high number of years between generations, and some of the dogs produced incorrect colors or other odd characteristics, indicating recent outcrosses. There also was the problem of Laverack sometimes giving different parents for the same dog. Stonehenge (Walsh), editorializing in the magazine *The Field*, questioned even the original source of the Laveracks.

This all needs to be viewed in context of the times however. Laverack began breeding his strain decades before there was any thought of establishing an official stud book, and all other pedigrees from the era come to a dead end at dogs with names like "Flash," "Nell," or "Lord so-and-so's Dog." Probably none can safely be taken at face value.

Pure strain or not, Laverack's setters were a definite type, and the fact remains that all successful English Setter lines to follow were based on them.

As an avid gunner, Laverack bred his setters for field work. He worked them from 9 a.m. to 7 p.m. daily for a 3-week season hunting grouse in the Scottish hills, and they were known for endurance. Laverack would hunt all day with a single dog, so he had good reason to proudly describe his setters as having "indomitable enduring, hard-working properties."

According to Argue, "Laverack shot all over the country on all sorts of ground, from the grouse moors of Perthshire to the blanket bogs of Caithness. He rented partridge shooting near my home at Tain, Easter Ross, and woodcock shooting in the coppiced oak woods of Argyllshire where his dogs were run with bells around their necks so they could be followed in close cover. He shot in Northern Ireland and he shot grouse and woodcock on the Isle of Islay, everywhere it seems, there was game that would lie to a dog's point."[1]

To illustrate his dogs' capabilities, in his book *The Setter*, Laverack wrote: " I will give an instance of the advantage of selecting good and lasting dogs. I was one of a party of four that on September 11th had bagged 3,066 head of grouse—one gentleman killed within seven head, to his own gun, as much as the whole party, solely by having superior dogs, and in addition, he lent a brace of dogs several times to his friends."[2]

Laverack touted his setters as having great natural instincts. "My breed hunt, range, point, and back intuitively at six months, and require comparatively little or no breaking." He famously wrote that with the assistance of a gamekeeper he "once broke eight dogs in six days; and all at the week's end were as steady as could be—pointing, backing, footing, and free from chase...I seldom use whip or whistle, but allow my dogs to use their own natural sagacity in making their casts and finding game."

This natural instinct and drive reportedly came at a price. Critics said Laveracks were difficult, headstrong, and almost unbreakable. Rev. D. W. W. Horlock gave a particularly interesting account:

> The ancient Laverack excelled in beauty, it also had surpassing good field qualities, a very high head, a wonderful nose, great pace, endurance, pluck, and a marvellous "sporting instinct." By this last is meant such a love for game-finding that it would go on for ever, even though never a bird was shot to it; but to all these qualities it added an almost invincible headstrongness and obstinacy, and this rendered it an impossible object of training to nine men out of ten, of that day at all events. So things happened thus: every one sought to cross his breed with a Laverack, of some sort or another, and everybody did it; and so a headstrong breed arose which no one could manage, and therefore men went out shooting without their dogs. [3]

By all accounts Laveracks were good looking dogs. Laverack described their appearance as that of a "strongly built spaniel." According to A. F. Hochwalt, they were "handsome, attractive animals, capable of winning anywhere on the bench." His and other descriptions of them were similar—small, heavily built, and low to the ground from a modern perspective, but elegant, and powerful in the field.

Few pure Laveracks were ever imported to America. Although the strain still predominated in the pedigrees, by the late 1800s most "Laveracks" were a mixture of British show lines. These dogs came over mainly as potential bench competitors, but they were also prized by American hunters, particularly grouse hunters. In his 1919 book, *The American Hunting Dog,* Warren H. Miller described Laverack setters: "And some of the best grouse dogs in the country have been straight Laveracks...Sir Roger, the Lingfields, the Alberts, the Queens,

Mallwyds, Wellingtons, Uhlans, Ch. Deodora-these are Laverack names that mean good grouse dogs as well as great bench winners."[4]

Llewellin

Richard Ll. Purcell Llewellin was one of the most successful breeders of Laverack-based English Setters of the late 1800s, sometimes called "improved Laveracks" at that time, and the only one to develop a distinct strain worthy of its own name. The Llewellins were pivotal in the formation of the modern English Setter, particularly in America.

The Llewellin strain was developed through crosses of pure Laveracks with three setters—Barclay Field's Duke, his sister Armstrong's Kate, and Thomas Statter's mixed breed female Rhoebe. Duke's pedigree is limited, but he was known to have descended from old English Setter lines. Some people questioned the authenticity of Kate's pedigree, but officially she was Duke's sister. Rhoebe was part Gordon Setter, part Southesk Setter, and rumored to carry other breeds. Various combinations of Duke-Rhoebe-Laverack bloodlines formed the basis of Llewellin's kennel, and the early American field trial setters.

The popular account of how Llewellin began is that he experimented for years (floundered, some said), first with Gordon and Irish Setters, and then Laveracks, trying various unsuccessful crosses between them before finally discovering the Duke-Rhoebe-Laverack cross in 1871. This persistent story was published at least as early as 1897 and has been re-written in various forms countless times since. Because Llewellin began breeding before registrations were the norm, it is impossible to confirm exactly when or how he started, but there is an extensive bench and field trial record to draw from. Those records establish that most or all of his experimentation occurred simultaneously and demonstrate the likely reason for Llewellin's success—he acquired and bred the best dogs available.

Llewellin won a small handful of show placements in the late 1860s with English Setters, and began competing seriously around 1870. His early field trial experience set the stage for the development of the Llewellins. The first trials Llewellin participated in were held at Shrewsbury in May 1870, where he entered three Gordon Setters. During his first year of competing the only win came from an Irish Setter named Plunket, a dog Llewellin purchased after being beaten by him at Shrewsbury.

Throughout the trials held that year Llewellin saw his Gordon and Irish Setters bested by dogs from all the lines that were to become the building blocks of the Llewellin strain—Garth's Laverack females Daisy and Bess, Field's Duke, and two stellar performances from a Rhoebe-Laverack male named Bruce.

At the spring 1871 Shrewsbury trials, one week after the second trouncing by Bruce, Llewellin purchased Statter's winning brace Dan and Dick. Like Bruce, Dan and Dick were out of Rhoebe, but they were sired by Field's Duke. Several of Duke's progeny were entered in the trials, and reported as "easily the best of the lot." As with Plunket the previous year, Llewellin bought the competition.

During this same period Llewellin acquired several Laveracks and began competing with them. At the fall 1871 Birmingham show, he won the championship class with Countess and the open for dogs with her littermate Prince. Countess won the same show the previous year with her first owner, and was considered by many to be the best Laverack to ever compete. She also convincingly won the all-age for bitches at the Vaynol trials in September, and with Plunket took the brace stakes. From the stud book report:

> The setters were a very good lot, Mr. Purcell Llewellin's brace, worked by Mr. Buckell, being about the best the Field reporter had ever seen, and even superior to Mr. Statter's Dan and Dick, purchased of Mr. Llewellin at Shrewsbury at a long price. He was so determined to have the best team possible, that he gave Mr. Statter 150£. for a half sister, Ruby, though not quite broken.[5]

The half sister Llewellin purchased for so much money was out of Rhoebe and Statter's Laverack male Fred. He also soon acquired a litter sister of Dan and Dick's named Dora. Llewellin now had in his kennel three of the five recorded progeny of the Duke x Rhoebe litter, and a Rhoebe-Laverack. His famous Irish-Laverack cross of Cora and Prince also occurred in 1871. During the next several years Llewellin bred and continued to compete with Irish Setters and straight Laveracks as he began producing Duke-Rhoebe-Laverack litters, the first of which were born in 1872.

Exports of Llewellins to America began almost immediately. Of the six dogs considered to have had the most influence on the early American field trial lines, five were from first generation Duke-Rhoebe-Laverack crosses. Gladstone, Leicester, and Lincoln were Dan-Laveracks, Druid was Dora x Prince, and Rake was out of Ruby x Dan. The last of the six, and probably the most influential of all, was Count Noble, out of a Dan-Laverack female named Nora. Count Noble's sire was Count Wind'em, a favorite of Llewellin's that was 75% Laverack and only one generation down from Dan x Countess.

Although derived from the same founding breedings, Llewellin's kennel and the American Llewellins did not stay on parallel paths. Llewellin linebred based on Duke-Rhoebe-Laverack crosses until his death in 1925, but unlike the Americans he selected for a homogenous conformation. Possibly also due in part to the supposition that Llewellin sent his culls to this continent, the American Llewellins quickly changed to something quite different than those he was breeding. Joseph A. Graham wrote:

> ...the typical American Llewellin cannot be understood without comprehending that the American type is widely different from Mr. Llewellin's ideals and from his own favorite dogs. He bred the ancestors, but he did not breed the type.[6]

That typical American Llewellin had been bred for, as Graham put it, "excellence not only of speed, but of performance at speed, which was new to the sporting world."

From the beginning, proponents of Laveracks and Llewellins, on both sides of the Atlantic, argued over which type was better, and which of the bloodlines Llewellin used contributed the most field abilities. Some critics wrote that Llewellin simply copied a cross originated by other breeders and then claimed the credit for himself.[7] Others said Llewellins were haphazardly bred, average setters loved only in America where they were foisted on gullible buyers. On the contrary, there were British writers like Horlock who thought Llewellin had a carefully developed breeding program that produced exceptional field and show dogs. At the same time, by reading various authors with differing values it becomes clear that Laveracks probably contributed much of the drive found in the better Llewellins, and that the early show lines derived from them were not as useless in the field as their critics claimed.

Disagreements like these surrounded English Setters well into the era of the early Rymans. If anything, at least in America, the acrimony escalated.

Count Noble at the National Bird Dog Museum in Grand Junction, Tennessee.

Am/Can Ch Rodfield, born in 1892. Dual Llewellin said to have looked like Gladstone. From *Field Trial Record of Dogs In America with other Authentic Statistics* by Maj. J. M. Taylor, Nickolson Printing Company, 1907.

Roots of the Rymans

George Ryman began breeding during a chaotic time in the American English Setter scene. It had been roughly four decades since the first Laverack and Llewellin imports. The Laverack type of English Setter had become the dominant show dog, and the Llewellins were the field trial strain. Controversy was raging over what an English Setter should be, with admirers of the two types in heated competition over which one should define the English Setter show standard. Not everyone in the setter world accepted this situation, and a brief delving into the history of the two types in America is necessary to understand the climate Ryman stepped into.

The oft-told version of how this "split" in English Setters came about is that field trial and show dogs were similar in the beginning and then went their separate ways. Books from the era, like Joseph A. Graham's 1904 *The Sporting Dog* and A.F. Hochwalt's 1919 *The Modern Setter*, sporting magazine articles, newspapers, and photos of the old dogs tell a story that is quite different. The two types certainly grew further apart over time, but the dogs never really were the same in America. What becomes apparent is that the true split was between the people involved in the breed.

The first of the Llewellins to come over was Dart, imported to Canada by L.H. Smith in 1874, followed in short order by others. This was also the year that the first bench show was held in America, and the year of the first field trial held by the Tennessee State Sportsman's Association in Memphis, Tennessee. Some of the early Llewellins were very successful in shows, easily besting the "native" setters already in America. Although there was great variation in their conformation, Llewellins were the premier show English Setters for a time.

The entrance of Llewellins in American field trials was at the second running of the Memphis trials in 1875, and it wasn't long before they were the predominant, winning strain in this arena of competition as well. Some of them also attained "dual" status—placements in both shows and field trials.

Gladstone and Count Noble, born in 1876 and 1879, were particularly influential in the development of Llewellins as field trial dogs. These two also made their mark on the conformation of the Llewellins, most notably Gladstone. Largely due to his fame as a field trial dog, and despite high ears, snippy muzzle, and overall a rather non show-like conformation, Gladstone won some placements in shows that predated the formation of the AKC, and like a few other Llewellins of the era was later awarded a championship retroactively.

Leicester, one of L. H. Smith's early show winning Llewellins. He was also one of the speediest of the day. Born in 1872, imported in 1875. From *The Dog Book*, by James Watson, Doubleday, 1906.

Because of their superior field qualities and the ability to pass them on to their descendants, Gladstone and Count Noble quickly became the dominant forces in the strain. They also passed on their less desirable conformation from a show perspective. Smith wrote in 1896, 22 years after he imported Dart:

> We have almost lost the Druid and Queen Mab type. Our best dogs of to-day show little of the long, narrow head and prominent skull, sudden stop and square muzzle, with long thin ear away down nearly on the neck, low. Body and crouching panther-like hind-quarters and long silky coat. These are the desirable points in a setter which so many animals from the first and second cross from the Laveracks had.[1]

Other writers from the 1890s mirrored Smith's lament. The majority of the Llewellins had been bred to what Joseph Graham called a "Gladstonian" type, intended to win American field trials of the era.

Charles H. Raymond imported the first pair of Laveracks, Pride of the Border and Fairy, the same year Dart came over, but Laveracks had a slower start in America than the Llewellins.

Am/Eng Ch Monk of Furness. Popular imported Laverack stud dog born 1885 in England. From *Kennel Secrets: How To Breed, Exhibit And Manage Dogs,* by Ashmont, 1904, Little, Brown, And Company.

Pride of the Border was a show winner and so were some of his offspring, particularly one of his sons, Thunder, who was nearly invincible in the ring. The better Laverack imports however began in the 1880s with dogs like Rockingham, Count Howard, and Monk of Furness. Often the dogs chosen for import had already won English championships and they were brought over to do the same in America.

Ch Highland Fleet. American bred Laverack owned by Dr. J. E. Hair. Born in 1896. From *Hearst International,* Vol 11, 1906.

Laveracks were never serious field trial competitors here but they were highly successful in the show ring despite being vastly outnumbered by Llewellins. By the end of the 1800s, they were beginning to take over. Of the 32 English Setter championships published in the AKC *Gazette* pre-1900, 12 were from straight or predominantly Laverack lines, 10 were Llewellins, and 10 were crosses of the two types.

Laveracks became even more dominant after a new wave of show imports began around 1900, exemplified by those from Thomas Steadman's Mallwyd kennel. These dogs, with their more refined head and body type were the beginning of the modern show setter, and they soon outclassed everything else in the ring. 51 English Setters won AKC show championships during the first

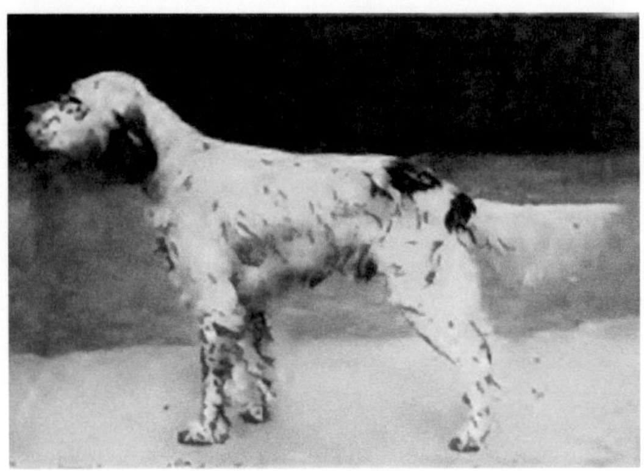

Ch Deodora Prince. Born in Scotland in 1901. Part of the second wave of Laverack types. From *Field Trial Record of Dogs In America with other Authentic Statistics* by Maj. J. M. Taylor, Nickolson Printing Company, 1907.

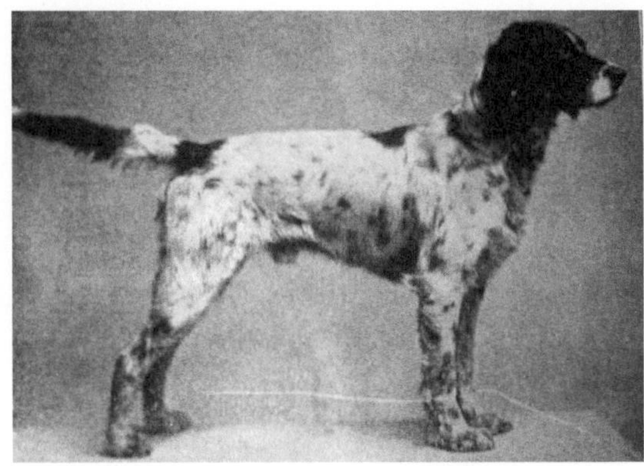

Field Ch Prince Rodney. Born in 1900. A. F. Hochwalt thought this dual Llewellin was a good example of a "medium type" of conformation. *Courtesy of American Field*

Field trial dogs occasionally won show championships as late as the 1920s. This was not because they looked like Laveracks, however (although a few did). Many people involved in the breed thought the English Setter standard should reflect a "utility" conformation—one that resulted in a dog with the speed and athleticism necessary to win field trials. Twice an English Setter Club was organized and an "American" standard written in an attempt to promote this type of setter. The first was in the early 1890s in response to the recent Laverack imports, the second in 1901. The conservative faction in the breed followed the British standard, which favored the Laveracks.

Judges who advocated both types were given their chance in the ring, with those who favored the Llewellins officiating more often in the West and South, frequently at shows held in conjunction with field trials. But even the Westminster show often alternated year to year to give judges from each side the opportunity to demonstrate their idea of what the standard should be. There was also an unsuccessful movement to bring the two extremes to what people like Hochwalt referred to as the "medium type"—a lighter more field capable dog that still had desirable conformation in the ring.

Arguments over the English Setter standard were a common subject in outdoor publications from the early 1900s. Numerous writers from every point of view complained about the inconsistent judging and/or poor quality of dogs being shown. The field people couldn't even come to agreement on how their standard should be interpreted. H.W. Huntington summed up the situation in this amusing piece published in *Outing Magazine* in 1901:

> The English Setter is deteriorating under the influence of uncertainty as to the kind of judge he will go before. A field trial judge sees "Hoodoo" win everything before him. "Hoodoo" is a big slashing dog, a rapid mover and a wide ranger; he fields all the birds, points and backs to perfection, and

Ch Sturdy Max winning best in show honors at the 1937 Morris and Essex, at that time the largest show ever held, with 4104 entries. This dog exemplified the shift in show conformation at the time of Rummey Stagboro, and for decades was considered the ideal to strive for. Born in 1932. From June 1937 *Kennel Club News.*

> mover and a wide ranger; he fields all the birds, points and backs to perfection, and wins, "hands down." He is a big slab-sided, splay-footed, raw-boned, heavy-headed, thick-skulled, long-backed dog, but in the field he certainly is a wonder. Presently this field trial judge is judging in the show ring, and he can see no dog in the class except "Hoodoo" so he gives him everything. A month later another judge officiates, at a show where the same dogs are entered. Then "Hoola Hoola" wins, a wastrel, little snipey-faced dog, with a greyhound head, short-backed as a pug, and as high on the leg as an ostrich—another type. And so it goes from show to show, until we have as many types of English setter as Joseph of old has colors in his coat.[2]

A few writers expressed optimism that the types would be brought together to one standard in the show ring. In 1911, after complaining about the quality of some of the Llewellins that had been shown over the years, Henry E. Parker wrote: "A happy medium is coming to the fore, a classic beauty, fine as a race horse, pleasing to the eye, but efficient and gluttonous when work comes along."[3] This optimism proved to be hopelessly unrealistic.

The split in the breed was not a new phenomenon in the early 1900s. The two types of setters were always different from each other. Graham wrote "In America the authentic history of the English setter is the history of the Llewellins, with the Laveracks appearing constantly in the bench shows and always disputing with the Llewellins the claim of correct type." and Parker "There has always been a distinctly marked difference between the bench strains and the field trial dogs..."

What was new was the rise and inevitable dominance of the Laverack types in the show ring, and the slipping influence of the field trial people. This dominance was ultimately cemented for good around 1930, in part by the appearance of the pre-potent sire Rummey Stagboro. The show breeders coalesced around the type of conformation he produced, and the English Setter Association was formed in 1931 as the only AKC recognized breed club.

There was now only one standard. The field people lost. To meet this standard they would have had to sacrifice performance and they abandoned shows altogether. Since then the two types have become even more specialized, and the schism in the breed has only widened.

A Third Type of English Setter

In the middle of all this was a movement to redefine the English Setter. The English Setter Club, formed by a group of Philadelphia sportsmen in 1906, was a prominent example (The name was changed to The English Setter Club of America in 1911, and later moved to Medford, New Jersey). Graham wrote about them: "The club is a new organization... whose object is to discover a type of setter which will have as much beauty as possible combined with the best ability in the field. They believe that bench shows have developed one extreme type, and field trials

Ch Hightone Tony. Dual Llewellin born in 1925. The last field trial English Setter to win an AKC show championship, awarded in June of 1929. *Courtesy of American Field*

another, neither being the dog which the amateur shooting man desires."[4] The club, which is still in existence today adopted the "American" standard, sponsored both shows and field trials, and was one of the five original Amateur Field Trial Clubs.

In the same article Graham went on to write "May be it must happen that the specialized dogs which score high in the ring must go one way, the racing, ranging field trial dogs another, and a third way be invented by the shooting men who do not care a rap for field trials and bench shows but want handsome dogs which can find birds in any cover and not demand a year's training before being decent to shoot over."

And then, prophetically:

> Some man will breed a recognized strain to please this third and largest class of sportsmen. It can be done by anyone who will ignore prize-winning fashions and stick to his object. Such a man must watch for the brains, looks and action of the dogs, and breed to the best.

To create this dog Graham proposed buying show setters with hunting abilities from breeders George Thomas, Charles Carter, or James Cole, and crossing them with Llewellins. He spelled out plans to try some crosses like this himself, and invited other breeders to do the same.

A well-known breeder who did try these crosses was George C. Thomas, Jr., one of the founders of the English Setter Club. He owned a number of famous show dogs, including champions Mallwyd Sirdar, Rumney Racket, and Madcap, and he experimented with Llewellin crosses to compete in field trials. In early 1907, Thomas sold his show dogs to his handler Ben Lewis. The *New York Times* called this "one of the most important deals in show dogs [English Setters were big news in 1907!]... Thomas has gone more into the line of breeding good-looking shooting dogs and the show canines not in keeping with the new idea have been disposed of in one lot..."

Numerous other breeders of the era crossed show and field lines, but often it is impossible to know for what purpose. In some cases, based on who the breeder was and the records of the dogs, the obvious intent was to win shows or field trials, and some of the crosses were influential in the development of the show lines. Others were advertised as shooting dogs. Whatever the purpose was, crosses of the two types appear somewhere in the background of virtually all modern show and field trial setters.

The breeders of these crosses, including Thomas, faded into obscurity. All but one. Only George H. Ryman emerged from this chaos to successfully create a third, recognized type of English Setter.

Foundation of the Rymans

George Ryman was successful where others failed in large part by insisting on an unusually high standard of quality. His experience as a market hunter, a professional trainer/handler, and a competitor in shows and field trials undoubtedly contributed to a unique level of expertise and ability to recognize the qualities he wanted in his setters. Ryman adhered to this high standard throughout his breeding career, but nowhere is it more obvious than in a study of the dogs he began with. They were setters that carried the foremost bloodlines of the time. A good place to start is with Sir Roger de Coverly, generally considered the fountainhead of the Rymans.

George Thomas's dog Mallwyd Sirdar was a major sensation in the show ring, and the first of the Mallwyds to be awarded an AKC championship. He is pictured in Graham's *The Sporting Dog* with the caption "...Laverack of a type admired by both fanciers and shooting men. Sirdar has an advantage over most Laveracks in free, strong movement. He has already sired a free-going young Laverack in Albert's Sirdar, and several really good field dogs from Llewellin dams. If any Laverack crosses well with American Llewellins it will probably be Mallwyd Sirdar." A litter whelped Jan. 18, 1907, out of one of these crosses produced Sir Roger de Coverly, bred by M. Mangan and owned by Dr. Horace M. Beck of Wilkes-Barre, PA.[5]

Sir Roger de Coverly's dam Lady Mangan was linebred to Field Trial Hall of Fame Ch Count Gladstone IV and carried lines to several other important early Llewellins, including Ch Lady's Count Gladstone and three great dual Llewellins—Ch Marie's Sport, Am/Can Ch Rodfield, and Field/Can Ch Antonio. Count Gladstone IV was out of a daughter of Gladstone bred to Count Noble, one of the classic founding American Llewellin breedings. Among other major placements he was the winner of the inaugural National Championship, and he produced winners with 21 different females.

Lady Mangan bred to Mallwyd Sirdar was a perfect example of the type of breeding Joseph A. Graham had envisioned, and dogs like Sir Roger de Coverly exemplified the movement to breed the shooting men's setters. His owner Dr. Beck, a member of the English Setter Club, campaigned a number of his setters in shows and trials. Although Beck was moderately successful with him, Sir Roger was somewhere between the two extreme types and could be considered a direct manifestation of the original ideals of the English Setter Club.

Among Ryman fans, Sir Roger has legendary status as the ultimate combination show, trial, and grouse dog. This legend probably originated with Beck, but Ryman certainly advanced it. His sales literature usually included "Ch Sir Roger De Coverly, winner of 63 Loving Cups in the field and on the bench." Sir Roger was not a champion (Ryman had a habit of giving a fanciful "Ch" to famous dogs mentioned in his sales lists) and he did not have anything like 63 first place wins, but his real record does reflect a competent field dog possessing excellent conformation.

Sir Roger's show record is that of a dog capable of being competitive in some venues, but not when up against the better Laveracks. He was most successful in the Field Trial Class, where he won a few firsts, including one at the 1915 Westminster. This class, which required at least one placement in a public trial, was not part of the competition for points toward a championship[6] and was typically dominated by Llewellins. Although Dr. Beck entered Sir

Roger in a few major shows, he was mainly campaigned in smaller local events, where he sometimes had little competition.[7] His placements at the Philadelphia Dog Show Association's February 1909 show were probably a good indication of his show quality. He won first in Novice Dogs and second in three other classes—Limit Dogs, Open Dogs bred in the US or Canada, and Open Dogs. The consistent second place wins suggest the judge thought Sir Roger was physically sound, but may have lacked that something extra that would have made him a stand out.

We have been able to confirm two trial placements for Sir Roger. He had one American Field recognized placement, a first in the 1911 Delaware Setter and Pointer Club's all-age stakes in a field of 19 starters, and he won the English Setter Club's all-age for dogs the same year, which at the time was a members-only stake.[8] Although these wins were not in major trials they are evidence that Sir Roger was probably a better dog in the field than he was in the show ring.

He may not have been a big winner, but Sir Roger de Coverly was not an obscure dog. A. F. Hochwalt, in his 1935 companion to *The Modern Setter,* wrote of having watched Sir Roger run in "very early one course trials of the east," and stated he was an excellent grouse dog (Hochwalt did not care for the way he moved however). Sir Roger also tops Warren H. Miller's list of best grouse dogs in his 1916 book *The American Hunting Dog.*

The records of Sir Roger de Coverly's offspring are another indication of his merit. Numerous females from various bloodlines were taken to him for stud service. These breedings produced two show champions, both owned by influential people in the English Setter scene. The first was Ch Meadowview Gleam O'Dawn, bred and owned by A. G. Hooley of the famous Meadowview Kennel in New York. The second, Ch Roger's Nola, was owned by Field Trial Hall of Fame member Frank Reily who along with Thomas headed the English Setter Club in its early days. Reily also owned a fantastic string of field trial dogs, including National Champion Eugene M.

The Cream of Setterdom, by V. E. Willoughby, credits Sir Roger with three field trial-winning offspring, one of which was Sir Roger de Coverly II. Three-quarters Mallwyd, and linebred to Mallwyd Sirdar, Sir Roger de Coverly II was the most famous of Sir Roger's offspring George Ryman owned. He produced three particularly notable Ryman setters. Bred to Blue Girl Jaine he sired prominent Ryman stud dog Sir Roger de Coverly II Jr and Ch King of Coverly, the lone show champion Ryman ever bred. He was also the sire of DeCoverly's Texas Queen, famous for being the grand dam of the only setter to win the National Championship three times, Field Trial Hall of Fame Ch Feagin's Mohawk Pal.

Ryman skillfully built on the reputation of the original Sir Roger de Coverly to create a legend around this bloodline. Although the most well known, the de Coverly's were only a part of the foundation of the Rymans, and to understand what Ryman did one must take a look at the background and people behind his other early dogs. Two prime examples are Ryman's Grouse Bill and Blue Girl Jaine.

Ryman's Grouse Bill was bred by field trialer Dr. W. F. Vail, of Greenwich, Connecticut. Bill's sire was Ben Tomahawk, from typical field trial lines, but his dam Gene Riley was anything but ordinary. Bred by Frank Reily, she was out of Jane Okaw and sired by Rod Sing. Rod Sing was one of Reily's better Llewellins from the Jessie Rodfield family. Jane Okaw's pedigree included some of the best of the early outcrosses from the Llewellins. Her sire Victor Okaw carried a show cross through the great dual setter Ch Cincinnatus Pride, plus a line to the "native" Campbell setters. Jane Okaw's maternal grand sire was May Fly, a dog imported in 1901. He was only half Llewellin, but he was a superb trial dog and produced well in England and in America. According to Hochwalt he contributed "bird sense, level-headedness, and size" when bred to the American Llewellins.

Blue Girl Jaine[9] is another great example. Her sire Wyoming Valley Mason was bred by H. M. Posten and E. B. Chase, two eastern Pennsylvania show breeders whose dogs were particularly prominent in early Ryman pedigrees. Posten and Chase both judged at shows, including Westminster. They bred setters individually, and together under the Wyoming Valley kennel name. Jaine's dam Princess West, owned by Robert West of Ashley, Pennsylvania, was from a fascinating mix of show and field trial lines. She was a granddaughter of Jessie Rodfield's Count Gladstone and also carried lines to Ch Marie's Sport and Oakley Hill. Her paternal grandparents were Ch Mallwyd Sirdar and Lady Cole. Owned by James Cole of Kansas City, Lady Cole was a wonderful Llewellin crossed show bitch, considered by some judges to be the most beautiful setter alive at the time.

Ryman used the finest of the show and field trial lines to create a new type of English Setter. Handsome dogs that excelled in the field, were specialized for hunting rather than competition, and filled the void that existed between the extremes required by the two competitive disciplines.

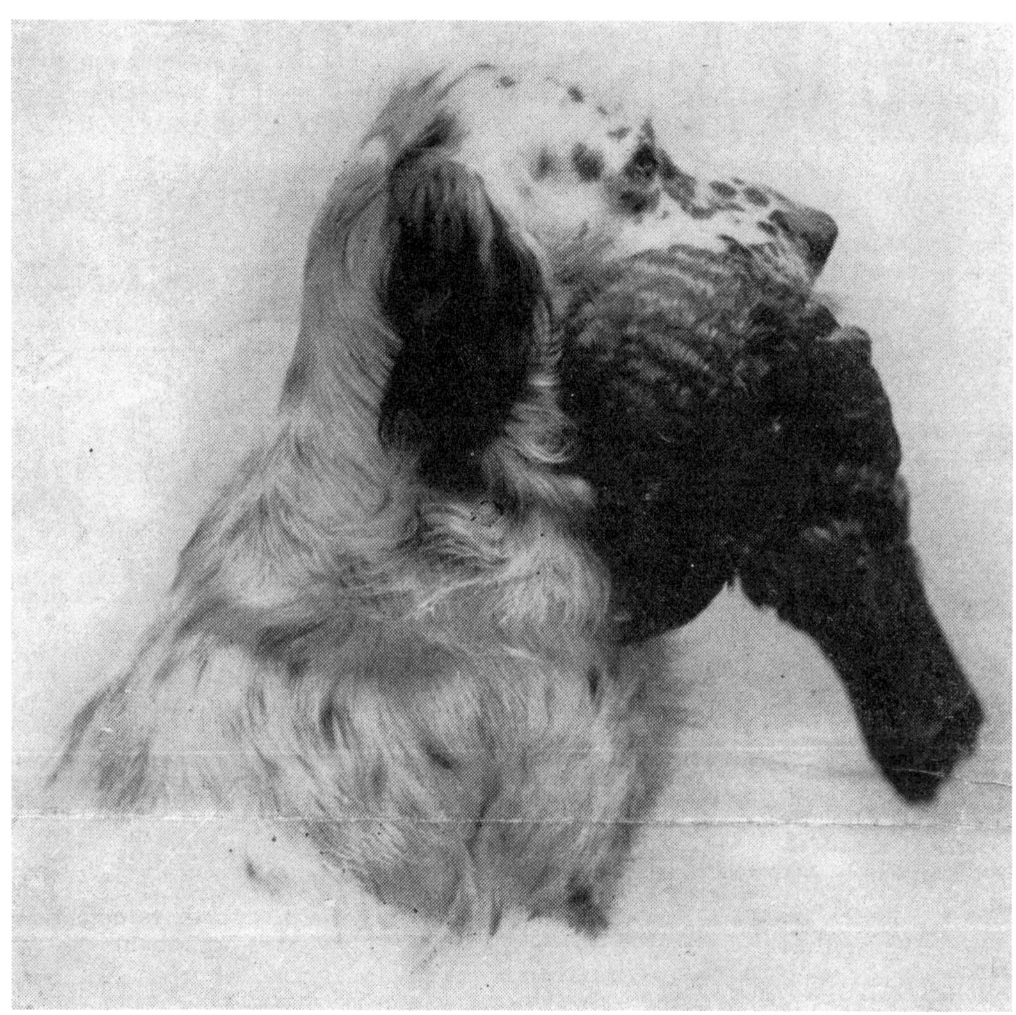

Sir Roger de Coverly II as pictured in Ryman sales literature.

A Calendar of Ryman Setter Breeding

The Ryman Pedigree Collection

The collection includes pedigrees that document the Ryman breeding program from its origins through Calkins breedings from the late 1960s. Most are the famous Ryman Gun Dog Kennels pedigree certificates that were presented to customers with the sale of the dogs. The collection also includes several American Field pedigrees, registration certificates, and two pedigrees from outside kennels. Images of the entire collection are included on *this book's companion CD.*

Examples of pedigrees are given here to guide the reader through a study of the breeding program. Most are part of the collection, but we have included a few additional early dogs to help give a more thorough picture of the beginnings of the kennel. We invite the reader to take the time to explore the entire collection. *Open the "index" file on the CD and scroll to "A Calendar of Ryman Setter Breeding." Click on the names of the dogs below to see their pedigrees as you read through the rest of this chapter.*

The Ryman Breeding Program

The Early Years: 1911 to 1929

SIR ROGER DE COVERLY II, 1911. The Rymans began here. Studbook records show that Ryman started building the foundation of the kennel with dogs whelped during the early teens. Among them were two offspring of Sir Roger de Coverly that were prominent in the early breeding program, Sir Roger de Coverly II whelped January 22, 1911[1], bred by H. M. Posten, and Ryman's Grouse Girlie whelped March 9, 1912, bred by Beck and Cox.

From Mallwyd show lines, with one quarter Llewellin through his grand dam Lady Mangan, Sir Roger de Coverly II had the looks and field abilities to build a reputation around. Ryman was in the thick of the movement to breed the "shooting men's" setters with Sir Roger de Coverly II. His success in the Pennsylvania grouse trials, which were instituted in 1913 to advance this type of dog, helped Ryman build his breeding program and promote Sir Roger de Coverly II as a popular stud dog. He could rightly be considered the true fountainhead of the Rymans.

It has been widely reported that Ryman bred to the original Sir Roger de Coverly and founded the kennel on those breedings. In a search of the studbooks we have found no record of Ryman ever breeding a female to Sir Roger de Coverly.[2] Although he appears somewhere in the background of a number of dogs Ryman used, the dominant source of Sir Roger de Coverly's bloodline was through Sir Roger de Coverly II.

Ch Mallwyd Sirdar. From *The Sporting Dog* by Graham

BLUE GIRL JAINE, 1912. A particularly important early Ryman female (highlighted in Chapter 6). Jaine's sire Wyoming Valley Mason was a cross of the older style of Laveracks with the Mallwyds. Her dam Princess West added the mixed background of exceptional show dog Lady Cole, plus excellent field trial lines through Pansey Rodfield. Note that Jaine was linebred to Ch Mallwyd Sirdar. Jaine was bred to multiple males in the kennel, most notably to Sir Roger de Coverly II, intensifying Sirdar's bloodline again and producing Sir Roger de Coverly II Jr.

RYMAN'S GROUSE TRAMP, 1913. Born May 9, 1913, Tramp is the earliest Ryman-bred English Setter we found in the Field Dog Stud Book. Tramp's sire Ryman's Staunch Bill was predominantly show line. His dam Blue Girl Dorothy was a full sister to Blue Girl Jaine. Dorothy was also bred to a Llewellin named Doctor Whitestone, which produced three dogs used in the breeding program.

RYMAN'S GROUSE BEAUTY, 1914. An early Ryman show dog. Ryman was active in shows during this time period. An example is the 1916 Gwynedd Valley Kennel Club Show, where he entered Beauty, her litter sister Ryman's Grouse Queen, and Sir Roger de Coverly II. Sir Roger de Coverly II did not place, but Ryman won first and second in the American Class with Beauty and Queen respectively, plus Beauty took Reserve Winner's Bitch. All three dogs were listed for sale at the show—the asking price for Sir Roger de Coverly II was $1000.

RYMAN'S MOHAWK PETE, 1916. Owned by A. G. White, of Toledo, Ohio, Pete was out of a Ryman breeding of strictly field trial lines. Pete's sire Ryman's Mohawk carried lines to a laundry list of famous Llewellins—within three generations are Ch Mohawk II, Tony Boy, Marse Ben, and Jessie Rodfield's Count Gladstone. Pete's dam Ryman's Miss Bloodstone carried a cross to the "native" Ethan Allin setters through the high-class field trial winner Colonel R, a dog that appears in a number of early Ryman pedigrees.

RYMAN'S GROUSE BILL, 1918. Bill's sire Ben Tomahawk was from excellent Llewellin lines, but, as noted in Chapter 6, the real highlights in his pedigree were on the dam's side—Rod Sing, May Fly and Victor Okaw. Victor Okaw was reportedly Frank Reily's favorite dog among the many greats he owned. Victor Okaw's dam was out of Brown's Queen Vic bred to dual dog Ch Cincinnatus Pride. Brown's Queen Vic carried the breeding of part Campbell female Daisy F to the Llewellin Gath's Hope, the most common source of the "native" Campbell bloodline in the field trial dogs. Although outcrossing from the Llewellins ultimately became an essential element in the development of modern field trial setters, at that time proponents of purity in the Llewellins wouldn't breed to dogs like Victor Okaw, known as "grades," so he was not used as much as he maybe should have been. Victor Okaw's questionable lineage certainly would not have been of any concern to George Ryman.

RYMAN'S GROUSE JOY, 1933. Joy's pedigree, and all those to follow are part of the collection. The pedigrees we chose to highlight here illustrate the direction of the breeding program and the more successful crosses that remained in the kennel. Through the 1920s the dominant feature of Ryman's pedigrees was the crossing of show and field lines. In a study of Joy's pedigree, one can begin to see how the early breeding program came together.

Joy's sire Ryman's Blue Grouse, whelped in 1927, was from predominantly Llewellin field trial lines mixed with the de Coverly bloodline. The field trial lines were through Ryman's Grouse Bill, Ryman's Grouse King (a show/field cross), and Superlative. Note that Superlative appears on both sides of Joy's pedigree. Bred by W. W. Titus, Ryman acquired this field trial winner in 1919 from Dr. W. F. Vail, the breeder of Ryman's Grouse Bill, and promptly won the Field Class at the Westminster show with him (and second place in 1920). Ryman advertised Superlative as "...the best Llewellin type in the country to-day."

On the dam's side of Joy's pedigree is a 1921 Ryman breeding of Superlative to a show bitch named Ryman's Miss Flo, which produced Superlative's Jean. Jean was the dam of show champion Albert's MacAllister II, whelped in 1925 and owned by Dr. J. E. Hair of Connecticut. Hair owned several of the top Laveracks of the late 1800s and early 1900s, and during the controversy over the English Setter show standard he was one of the main proponents of the British standard. There are Albert's dogs in the background of many early Rymans, all of which were from Hair's kennel.

DUKE OF DECOVERLY'S, 1935. Ryman's Grouse Dorothy, on the sire's side of this pedigree, was out of a good example of an early Ryman breeding from 1922, Sir Roger de Coverly II Jr x Hardscrabble Judy. Hardscrabble Judy carried some of the finest field trial lines of the era through Lady Quail P, plus lines to prominent early show dogs Am/Eng show Ch Mallwyd Edward, and Am/Eng Ch Mallwyd Invader. Note that Dorothy was bred to Ryman's Blue Grouse to produce Roger DeCoverly Pete, a Ryman stud dog linebred to Sir Roger de Coverly II Jr. and roughly half field trial, half show.

Born in 1916, Sir Roger de Coverly II Jr was an important stud dog in the early breeding program, siring litters for Ryman as late as 1927. He did not have any American Field recognized wins himself, but he produced three offspring with seven placements between them, bred and owned by Dr. Beck and whelped May 4, 1921 out of Beck's Peg O'My Heart.

1930s

Show lines became more prominent in the breeding program during the 1930s. Most notably Ryman owned four dogs from the famous and highly successful show breeding of Rummey Stagboro to Lakelands Nymph. Although the direction of the breeding program was more toward show lines, Ryman did continue to add field trial lines to the kennel during the 1930s.

RYMAN'S DUAL JIM, 1932. Dual Jim was a stud dog out of Rummey Stagboro and Lakelands Nymph. Rummey Stagboro was the most influential dog ever in the development of the show lines, and he represented an important outcross from the American show dogs through his sire Spiron Jagersbo. Spiron Jagersbo's dam was predominantly Llewellin and his sire was Swedish Ch Spiron. Lakelands Nymph was roughly one quarter Llewellin and also carried superb show lines. Rummey Stagboro x Lakelands Nymph was a very significant breeding, and remains famous eighty years later. The fact that Ryman owned four of the offspring demonstrates his ability to recognize superior quality and his determination to acquire the best of the best.

Ryman entered Dual Jim and two other dogs in the 1937 Morris and Essex show (the only time Rymans were ever entered in this show). Presumably Dual Jim had the potential to be competitive, but all three were marked as absent at the show.

RYMAN'S CANADIAN ROY, 1933. This pedigree is a good example of a straight show breeding. The dam, Ryman's Dual Arline, was one of the Rummey Stagboro x Lakelands Nymph dogs. The sire, Trevallen Ben, was a Canadian show setter from excellent lines. Ryman used a number of Canadian imports in his breeding program.

RYMAN'S SHOHOLA BELLE, 1935. Belle's dam was Racket's Joan D. The "D" setters were from the famous show kennel of Dr. W. F. Daw in Vancouver, BC. In his 1951 book *The Complete English Setter* Davis Tuck highlighted the superb hunting abilities of Racket's Joan D's half brother Ch Jiggs Mallwyd D. Joan D was bred to multiple males in the kennel, in this case Ryman's Dual Jim.

DUKE OF DECOVERLY'S, 1935. Duke was a prominent Ryman stud dog. His sire, as mentioned above, was one of Ryman's classic mixes of show and field lines. His dam Queen of MacAllister carried show lines through Albert's MacAllister, Sir Roger's Emms, and Mallwyd Grant[3]. She also brought in a

Top producing field trial dog Sport's Peerless. *Courtesy of American Field*

number of field trial lines that included Ch Phil's Speed Ben and Ch Mohawk Whitestone. Duke was a quintessential Ryman blend of both types of setters.

RYMAN'S GROUSE FOX, 1936. This pedigree contains Ryman's well known cross to field Ch Nugym, through Fox's sire Governor Penn. Governor Penn also carried lines to several other important field trial dogs, including National Ch Eugene M., Ch Riley Frush, Ch Prince Rodney, and Ch Lamberton's Mack. He was a full sibling of Rod's Lady Bird, the dam of influential field trial dog Sam L's Skyrocket. Fox's dam Ryman's Blue Racer was from strictly show lines.

RYMAN'S STYLISH LADY, 1937. A straight show dog, Lady introduced lines to Ch Gore's Blue Pal, and Am/Eng Ch Pennine Patron among others.

ELLIS'S ROYAL SALUTE, 1939. Royal Salute was an important show line stud dog in the kennel. Imported from Canada.

SHOHOLA FALLS HIGH, 1939. A pivotal event in the breeding program begins here. George Ryman's famous cross to Field Trial Hall of Fame and top producing field trial dog Sport's Peerless began in 1939 with breedings to his son Sport's Peerless High. Ryman wrote regarding these breedings, "It was what I wished for and hoped to get back in the good English Setter for many years." This ultimately proved to be Ryman's most successful cross.

1940s

Ryman returned to his roots during the 1940s and brought more field influence back into the breeding program, chiefly through the Sport's Peerless cross. Among several sons and grandsons of Sport's Peerless that Ryman tested as potential sires, by far the best producer was son Sport's Peerless High. Another son, Peerless Seneca Boy, was also successful as a sire, along with a grandson named Director.

DIRECTOR, 1940. Son of Field Trial Hall of Fame National Ch Sport's Peerless Pride, Director also carried lines to many other great field trial dogs, including Ch Riley Frush, Florendale Lou's Beau, and Vic O'Crahu.

Director won two American Field recognized trial placements before Ryman acquired him, including a first as a derby, handled by his breeder W. B. Propes. He was later sold to R. J. Andrews and won two more placements handled by Frank Lemons. Ryman used the field trial records of dogs like Director as a selling point (often exaggerated; he claimed "several firsts" for Director), but trialing was not an important part of Ryman's evaluation of his dogs. Willoughby's book *The Cream of Setterdom*, which is a fairly comprehensive record of American Field recognized trial placements through 1945, lists only a handful of placements by Rymans, none of which were owned or handled by Ryman except Sir Roger de Coverly II.

SPORT'S BEDSIDE MANOR, 1940. A son of Sport's Peerless, Ryman changed the name of this dog to Peerless Maywood, and he sired at least one registered litter. Ryman wrote that he purchased five additional sons of Sport's Peerless following the initial success with Sport's Peerless High. Of them one was a "wonder" as a sire, one was "fair," and the other three were "useless." Peerless Seneca Boy was bred multiple times and was likely the wonder. Peerless Maywood may have been the fair sire. We have not seen Ryman-registered litters sired by any other sons of Sport's Peerless, but there was one sired by an additional grandson named Sport's Peerless Zephyr (also in the collection).

RYMAN'S GROUSE PRIDE, 1942. This is a good pedigree to see how crosses to Sport's Peerless began to be used in the kennel. In this case Sport's Peerless High was bred to Shohola Falls Rubby, a predominantly show line female. Field trial dogs in her pedigree were Cuban Maid and Alice Elizabeth R. Rubby also carried the early Ryman breeding of Superlative to Ryman's Miss Flo.

RYMAN'S RACKET BOY, 1942. Racket Boy was a prominent stud dog in the kennel out of Ryman's show lines. He was bred to various females, often those carrying a Sport's Peerless cross.

RYMAN'S GROUSE FORTRESS, 1943. Fortress was sired by Duke of DeCoverly's and out of Ryman's Grouse Gladys. Gladys, sired by Sport's Peerless High, was reportedly Ryman's all-time favorite dog.

FANNING'S LARRY JOE, 1944. Fanning's Larry Joe was one-quarter field trial through his paternal grand sire Grace's Beau, and he carried exceptional show lines. A highlight on his dam's side is the great Ch Daro of Maridor, the single English Setter to ever win Best of Show at Westminster, bred to top producing bitch Lutta of Delwed. Daro was out of Ch Sturdy Max, one of the best offspring of Rummey Stagboro, and one of the best show dogs ever. Of interest, the breeding mentioned previously of Sir Roger de Coverly II Jr. to Beck's Peg O'My Heart is in Sturdy Max's background through Ch Pat II.

Ryman used several show line stud dogs whelped in the early 1940s, but new show crosses disappear from the pedigrees by the middle of the decade, and the show lines introduced through Fanning's Larry Joe were some of the latest to come into the breeding program. This correlates well with the end of the field influence in shows just over a decade earlier. Show lines Ryman already had remained very influential in the kennel, but he clearly became less interested in new show dogs and expressed dissatisfaction with their performance in the field. He did not give up on them entirely however, as he later owned, but never used, a show champion whelped in 1950 named Hadceda Cavalier.

RYMAN'S SENECA GIRL, 1946. Seneca Girl was featured prominently in the kennel's sales literature. She was sired by Peerless Seneca Boy out of show bitch Ryman's Stylish Lady.

Ryman's Seneca Girl as she appeared in Ryman sales literature.

RYMAN'S BIRDY CLIP, 1948. Clip's sire Byrnes Blue Duke was another Canadian born stud dog, whelped in 1944. He carried the same show lines as Ellis's Royal Salute, plus field trial lines through Peerless Queen's Lady and Ellis Bonnie Bess.

Early 1950s

The late 1940s and early 1950s are considered by most to be the height of the kennel. The Sport's Peerless cross was instrumental in developing the greatest era of the Rymans. Descriptions, sales lists, and photos paint a picture of the typical Ryman from this period as a 50 to 60 lb. male or 45 to 50 lb. female that was athletic, stylish and naturally talented in the field, possessed much of the good looks of Ryman's show lines, and was a fine personal companion.

RYMAN'S ORANGE BEAU, 1950. Ryman continued to bring new field trial blood into the breeding program. Beau's sire Ryman's Peerless Beau carried lines to a number of important field trial dogs, including Sam L's Skyrocket, Equity, and Florendale Lou's Beau.

RYMAN WHITE'S FRIENDSHIP, 1951. This pedigree, roughly 70 percent show lines and 30 percent field trial lines, is typical for the early 1950s. Sport's Peerless High appears on each side of the pedigree, along with Director on the dam's side. Ryman's pedigrees had a fair amount of this type of relatively distant linebreeding, but he did not breed a true "line" of setters in the classic sense.

RYMAN'S BLUE SKY X RYMAN'S BLUE SUE, 1953. Another pedigree showing the influence of Sport's Peerless High. In this breeding we can also see the Rummey Stagboro x Lakelands Nymph influence, the Canadian show dogs, the Nugym cross, and lines to Ryman's original show/field crosses.

RYMAN'S BLUE WIF, JANUARY 12, 1955. Wif is the latest pedigree in the collection that lists George Ryman as the breeder.

This is the end of the George Ryman era. In 1955 Ryman suffered a stroke, and by necessity his wife Ellen took over the breeding program.

RYMAN'S MISS GAIL, JULY 3, 1955. The first pedigree in the collection that shows Ellen Ryman as the breeder.

Post 1955

George Ryman died in 1961. Ellen Ryman operated the kennel on her own until she married Carl Calkins in 1963. The breeding practices changed dramatically after Ryman's stroke. Realistically, Ellen could not have duplicated George Ryman's evaluations of the dogs and search for new bloodlines by herself. Just keeping the kennel running would have been a tremendous effort for her. Even after Carl Calkins came on board outcrosses from the lines already in the kennel were rare, and the Calkins' selected for a different type of setter than Ryman preferred.

RYMAN'S BLACK PATCH, 1965. A typical Calkins era pedigree. Until the fifth generation every dog was out of a Ryman to Ryman breeding. It isn't until the sixth generation that outside dogs really become evident, all from the George Ryman era.

RYMAN'S BOLD RETURN X RYMAN'S SHOHOLA PRIM, 1966. Bold Return was a prominent Calkins stud dog.

SIR LOUIS LYONS X RYMAN'S DECOVERLY MADAM. This was an outcross the Calkinses did use. Sir Louis Lyons was part Ryman and carried a number of field trial lines. The breeding produced Ryman's DeCoverly Dandy, a dog that can be found in many later pedigrees.

RYMAN'S DECOVERLY J X RYMAN'S AUTUMN WHISPER, 1969. The latest pedigree in the collection.

One can only speculate where Ryman himself would have taken the breeding program if he had lived longer, but by all accounts the majority of the dogs became significantly larger and slower in the field under the Calkinses. The changes in the dogs and the breeding practices during the Calkins era, along with the passage of time, lead to a modern misconception of what Ryman's dogs really were. A person whose introduction to the kennel came in the late 1960s or early 1970s might not even recognize some of the smaller more athletic setters from the 1950s as Rymans. Although many people found the larger dogs from the Calkins era to be more desirable, and still do, they were far removed from the English Setters of George Ryman's masterful blending of show and field lines.

PART IV BREEDING THE APPALACHIAN RYMAN SETTER

The really essential things one must teach a pup are not so numerous as some suppose. He must be gifted with a good nose and he must, sometimes, be taught staunchness. With these two, fundamental virtues he will become a valuable asset to your hunting,—if he has been blessed with a modicum of brains

---

Quite often the trouble lies not with the dog but with the handler. It is not unusual to see a man who should know better, hold his dog with loud and strident demands of 'To-Ho,' when a novice could see, by the dog's attitude and eagerness to go on, that he was no longer getting scent

—Burton L. Spiller,
Grouse Feathers, 1947.

H. Burnell Davis with an Alder Run pup.

Our Circle of Breeders

It was at a small gathering of Ryman setter owners in Pennsboro, West Virginia, when one fellow announced that we should keep these bloodlines to ourselves, covet them, and not allow others to share our wealth. This provincial way of thinking did not appeal to Burnell Davis, who vehemently let it be known that this would be a major mistake. We had to keep our eyes open, breeding only the best to the best, and do everything we could to maintain these bloodlines by line breeding as much as possible. Burnell encouraged me to check out every dog advertisement we ever saw with the word "Ryman" in it. I didn't realize it at the time but Burnell was trying to get us to pursue a breeding program not too unlike that of George Ryman's. Not that Ryman line bred his setters all that much; we know that he did a lot of out crossing throughout his career, but always had in mind a particular type in regard to how the dogs should look and how they should perform in the field.

George Hanson and I were the other members present at this gathering and, both of us being very new to this endeavor, but I listened carefully to what Burnell had to say. It sounded to be the most reasonable approach to a breeding program and, after all, Burnell was the old master...there was no question about that in our minds. What he said made a lot of sense to me and, being young at the time, I was highly inspired about anything Burnell told me about the Ryman setters.

I met George Hanson while seated in a small restaurant in Middlebourne, West Virginia, shortly after I started working. I remember a young, shy, blond-haired fellow who my district biologist supervisor and I invited to have lunch with us. The shyness part will come as a complete surprise to those who only knew George later in life. It was me who had to approach a landowner to ask permission for fishing or hunting access. Both of us were newly employed by the same state agency (different sections since George was a fisheries biologist and I, a wildlife biologist) and, coming from out of state, we were not completely accustomed to the ways and manner of mountain folks. It didn't take us long to adapt to the mountains and their people.

George soon got involved with running and breeding Treeing Walker Coonhounds and developed a West Virginia Night Champion—Mountain State Bawling Bowser was his name. George also was very interested in bird hunting, and purchased a setter pup from the first litter I bred. This was Alder Run Dawn—a full sister to Starr—the pup I kept for myself from this same litter (Ryman's Sky Joe x Ryman's Blue Heather). George would either hunt 'coons or run dogs at night and hunt birds in the daytime—when he wasn't working, of course. It didn't take him very long to look like a walking skeleton!

George encouraged me to 'coon hunt... not having pursued this activity in the past, I jumped right in and bought half interest in two hounds with another friend. I found that I couldn't hunt all night and spend the following day looking for dogs. It interfered with available time for my family, setters, and bird hunting.

We both hunted and ran dogs with Burnell at times—many times, in my case. This gave Burnell the opportunity to observe both Dawn and Starr in the grouse woods. Burnell was convinced we were on the right track and urged us to continue line breeding these bloodlines. He was my primary mentor and my advisor when it came to managing the setters. In my mind, no one knew these Ryman dogs, and setters in general, as well as Burnell. He raised a couple litters by taking Ryman's Blue Heather after she was bred, and taking a pup for himself. He and I would travel to Canaan Valley to expose our setters to woodcock during early gunning season and stay over at the Worden's hotel in Davis. Bud Evans joined us at least one of those years.

George and I advanced in our careers and both of us moved to other parts of the Mountain State; but our families were close and we did stay in touch with dog breeding matters and even got together on a hunt once in a while.

George worked closely with Bob Sumner after Dave Francis purchased the initial Ryman setters from Ellen and Carl Calkins. At the time, Bob was manager of their shooting preserve at Kathy's Farm. George also maintained a consulting relationship with Bob after the purchase of the remaining setters and the movement of Ryman kennels to Hillsboro, West

H. Burnell Davis examining Alder Run Starr's Litter.

George Hanson and two of his setters.

Virginia. This arrangement gave both men an opportunity to study George Ryman's pedigrees and breeding program. The pedigrees came along with the purchase of the Ryman setters. I do not know what was lost in the abandonment of the Hillsboro Ryman Setter operation, but I felt very fortunate in being able to acquire the collection of pedigrees, which later revealed the entire Ryman setter breeding history. I found it exciting just to thumb through the pedigrees from time to time.

As I have explained elsewhere, I was discouraged after seeing the seventy dogs purchased from Carl and Ellen Calkins—especially after viewing the assortment of dogs used by Bob Sumner as breeding stock. After seeing these dogs, I was convinced the Ryman setter, as developed by George Ryman, was lost, except perhaps for some of the older bloodlines we were maintaining. If anyone else had this early Ryman blood, I was not aware of it. I knew at that point I had to be looking elsewhere for breeding material, except for breeding back to Bob's Shadbush Ryman's Ruff.

George had been more aggressive with his breeding program than I, especially with his willingness to outcross. Perhaps the best outcross George made, in my opinion, was to Queen's Widmont Jo-Jo owned by George's good friend, Dana Chalfant of Pittsburgh. George bred Jo-Jo to his Farm Girl Rose. Rose was out of Shadbush Ryman's Ruff and Kathy's Devil Ann—the latter being from those dogs originally purchased from the Calkins by David Francis and managed by Bob Sumner. Jo-Jo's sire was Seneca Grouse High out of Old Hemlock Jeb and Alder Run Dawn. His dam, Chante Bleau was completely of field trial blood with names such as Flight Commander, Turnto, Glencrest Doctor, Beau Essig and Skyrocket. Therefore Jo-Jo was one-half Ryman and one-half field trial lines.

Although George lived only a few miles away, I purposely delayed seeing the litter out of Jo-Jo and Farm Girl Rose until they were close to weaning age, when Ellie and I stopped off at George's farm to see the pup he had selected for me. I had previously told George that I wanted a female from this litter, but was completely unsatisfied with his selection of "my" pup. There was a lot of conformation variability in this litter due to the outcross. So much variation that I told George at the time, "there is only one pup I would take out of this litter—that full-masked tricolor—he is beautiful!" George's reply was "you can't have him—he's been promised to a fisheries biologist in Pennsylvania." I declined from taking any other pup from this litter. On our way home, Ellie, who had not been in on our discussion of the pups, but had seen the female George picked out for me, commented; "you're not going to take that pup, are you?" She always did have a good eye for dogs.

When that litter was 6-months of age, George called to ask me if I would still take that tricolor pup, since the other arrangement for his placement had fallen through the cracks. I immediately accepted the offer and dropped everything to go and pick up "Dawn's Shadbush Ted," who not only was a very fine gun dog with a most unique personality, but also the sire of many fine pups that turned into good gun dogs.

Kay and Bert Pierce are the next to enter the Appalachian Ryman setter breeding scene. They started grouse hunting in West Virginia with a small poodle. Bert, being a fisheries biologist employed by the state, had connections with George Hanson and thereby acquired a setter from George by the name of "Little Dawn." These folks are very serious about their grouse hunting. Kay hunts longer and harder than most of the male hunters of about the same age I knew! Kay has been the manager and handler of the setters in

Hunter Lesser showing Shadbush Ryman's Ruff, by Ryman's Mike Blue and Alder Run Dawn. Owner: Robert E. Sumner.

that family, taking a deep interest in the continuation of the bloodlines we possessed. They have literally lived with their dogs—even to the point of taking them along while fishing. Kay has had an excellent eye when it comes to judging the Ryman setter—especially in regard to conformation, style, and ability as grouse dogs. I attribute much of the progress we made in maintaining the Ryman setter to Kay's work in the breeding program.

In Kay's own words:

> Our first English setter, "Little Dawn," came to our home as a replacement for a 9-pound Toy Poodle who was our first dog. Other than sleeping in an outdoor kennel, as advised by other pointing dog owners, Little Dawn experienced the same life style as a house pet. We found that, contrary to most of the literature about pointing dogs, Little Dawn was a great companion. She was our first duck hunter, being very content to sit in a blind and alerting us to incoming ducks with a sharp turn of her head in the right direction. Her love of duck hunting began the tradition of using our succeeding setters for waterfowl dogs who love going in the boat as much as the truck. It has been a fascination to witness "the desire to please" which allows these dogs to learn easily.
>
> Fishing trips are not just for anglers. Whether it is crappie, bass, or walleye on a local lake, or a float trip in a Jon boat or inflatable canoe, there is always a setter at the helm. They don't insist on going for just the ride. Each fish caught is pointed. The mere reaction by the fisherman to a strike brings a response of "get ready" by getting in position to point it. If the strike is missed, there is obvious disappointment by angler and dog. The fish are greeted with a little chase around the live well, and then back into position for another one. If one angler is catching more fish than the other, they can expect to have a dog very close by.

Kay had Misty Meadows Brooke, an excellent grouse dog bred by George Hanson (Kathy's Farmboy Pete x Tomboy's Dew Drop), who we bred to Ted. Of the six pups whelped, Kay kept one she called "Brooke's Shadbush Whit." Another one of these pups was placed with Herbert "Buck" Ratliff, of the same school of grouse hunting and both Buck and the Pierces lived just outside of the same central West Virginia town of Gassaway. Buck's setter was "Brooke's Shadbush Zeb." I spent some very special hours with Buck and the Pierces in the Mountain State grouse woods.

Kay and I spent a couple enjoyable years judging "Shoot-To-Retrieve" field trials in central West Virginia. We rode behind each brace of dogs using small hunting-type mules—the kind that are transported by pickup truck. Unmounted, they jump into the truck bed and are commonly used in the mountains by bear hunters. The mules are broken to gunfire and are, most of the time, a pleasure to ride—so I discovered. I found it interesting to ride behind the braces of running dogs, observing their actions, and that of their handlers.

The mules generally were more considerate of their riders than horses, in my experience. It was sometimes difficult getting them to move after standing in place for a while, but a switching would get the mule in motion—usually with a quick start!

For the most part our mules were gentle and did not aggressively react to gunfire or dogs; with only one exception. A German short-haired pointer was allowed to get a little too close for my mule's comfort, causing the mule to rear up in her attempt to strike the pointer with her front legs. I didn't know the mule could move that fast! I quickly called for the handler

Kay Pierce taking a grouse from her Brooke's Shadbush Whit, (Dawn's Shadbush Ted x Misty Meadows Brooke).

Walt and Kay judging at a Shoot-To-Retrieve field trial.

to remove his dog whereby the mule settled down, back to normal.

Neither Kay nor I had been certified as National Shoot -To-Retrieve judges and, as time went on, the pressures to undergo our certification requirements and travel became greater, so we both decided to leave the judging to others. I was, however, glad that I had the experience of taking part in these trials and I'm certain Kay felt the same way.

Buck's setter Zeb had a marvelous field trial record in these local "Shoot-To-Retrieve" events.

Buck and I "traded" grouse and woodcock covers in the mountains of West Virginia. We also took some trips together to states like Idaho, where we hunted two species of prairie grouse, Blue grouse and Ruffed grouse. In Wisconsin, we hunted grouse and woodcock with Cliff and Lisa Weisse.

Buck Ratliff is applauding Brooke's Shadbush Zeb for the retrieve of his grouse. (Dawn's Shadbush Ted x Misty Meadow's Brooke).

Hunting with Buck, there was one certainty—we were going to take advantage of every possible ray of available light, and we were going to walk a lot! He was a good grouse hunting buddy. The walking didn't bother me even though I was 20 years Buck's elder.

All my hunts with Buck were memorable, but there was one in particular that stood out. We were in one of West Virginia's remote heavily cut-over areas, working two dogs at a time, each with one of our own. Grouse numbers were reflective of the great looking habitat we were hunting and the setters were handling just the way they should. It was one of those evenings when everything fell in place. It was late dusk and we still hadn't made it to my vehicle when my orange Belton setter, LeftiK, pointed while "buried" in a very dense pile of treetops. I rarely have trouble getting to a dog on point but, in this

Buck Ratliff holding Shadbush Chessie (Alder Run Theodore x Brooke's Shadbush Whit).

poor light, I could not find a way into this pile of woody debris. Maybe I was just too tired! Buck approached LeftiK from the opposite side of the cover where he had some opening, flushed the grouse, and fired. All I could see was the fire coming from his double. I asked if he needed a retrieve since I figured LeftiK didn't stand a chance of seeing the bird. Buck answered that he did not know if he had hit it and that it flew in the direction of our truck. All we knew to do was continue in that direction. I watched LeftiK as he left the cover and headed down the bank toward the road. He stumbled on a very dead grouse lying in the road ditch, picked up the bird, and proudly delivered it to me.

On the way out, driving down the road in total darkness, Buck announced: "we never took a picture—you might get killed driving home and we will not have a photo of this great hunt, and the five grouse we're taking out of this place." I immediately swung the vehicle into a gas well opening, lined up the dogs with Buck, set the camera on self timer and placed it on the hood of the vehicle. We had our printed memory of this great grouse hunt!

Buck was killed in a tractor accident in the late summer of 2009, while carrying out a wildlife management activity on his property in Braxton County. I attended the very crowded wake and placed two grouse tail feathers, from a male and female, in Buck's shirt pocket.

Billie Paxton with her setter Paxton's Rex Spartacus (Dan's Wooly Tricolor x Alder Run Shadows).

I wanted to be certain there was a grouse population where Buck was going.

Billie Paxton, of Elkview, West Virginia, developed a fine stud dog in Paxton's Rex Spartacus, by breeding Dan's Wooly Tricolor, owned by Dan Cantner, to Alder Run Shadows. Billie bred her setters to my male, Dawn's Shadbush Ted, multiple times and also to Alder Run LeftiK, thereby producing more of this line.

Spartacus was bred to Alder Run Tara (Dawn's Shadbush Ted x Alder Run Heather) to produce Alder Run LeftiK. LeftiK, being a prepotent sire and very desirable setter—from a conformation and hunting viewpoint—was bred to numerous bitches. Among those using him as a stud were: Dr. Max Sponseller of Georgetown, Delaware; Walter A. Saling, Jr. (Grouse Woods Setters) of Ligonier, Pennsylvania; and Preston Faust of Hiltons, Virginia.

Dr. Sponseller bred his Cokesbury's Autumn Mist to LeftiK and continued with these bloodlines through her progeny. Walt Saling bred his Grouse Woods Dyna to LeftiK, and later bred Grouse Woods Skye to Shadbush Lancelot. Preston bred Ryman's Blue Girl to LeftiK and Ryman's Orange Ginger to Dawn's Shadbush Ted.

Ryman's Grouse Winston, (Ryman's Bold Return x Ryman's Golden Penny), owned by Victor N. Green of Charleston, West Virginia, was bred to Alder Run Pixie (Ryman's DeCoverly Pride x Alder Run Starr) by Phyllis J. Thomas of

Walt Saling and a litter of Grouse Woods Setters, September 1995– Grouse Woods Skye X Grouse Woods Jock. *Photo by Sandy Layton.*

Sissonville, West Virginia. The crosses made by Billie and Phyllis contributed to the furtherance of this line of setters.

There were other breeders to these males, but I had to stop somewhere and choose to do so immediately after the early breeders of these Appalachian Rymans.

Cliff and Lisa Weisse who own and operate the October Setters Kennels in Island Park, Idaho, stopped at our Elkins home in pursuit of a Ryman stud dog. At the time they owned two setters that carried our Appalachian Ryman lines, plus a female descended from the later Ryman bloodlines named Holly. The Weisses had sought me out because they liked what they saw in the early bred Ryman bloodlines and were interested in my stud LeftiK. When I found out where they lived in Idaho, I suggested they contact Dr. Fred Hyde in Pocatello—only 100 miles from Island Park—who owned a son of LeftiK's. The Weisses bred October Mountain Holly to Alder Run Rummy, which was the beginning of their breeding program. No one is more familiar with the characteristics and makeup of original Ryman setters than Lisa, who has studied George Ryman's breeding program intensively. Cliff and Lisa work their setters regularly on Ruffed grouse and woodcock as well as prairie grouse, chukar and Hungarian partridge, insisting on close working, but athletic dogs having the appearance of the early Rymans.

In Cliff and Lisa's own words:

We were introduced to Ryman setters by long time grouse hunter and friend, Bill Ingraham. Bill tells a story of driving down Main Street in Georgetown, Massachusetts, one day and seeing a man with a beautiful orange belton setter on the sidewalk. He made a quick U-turn and went back to find out what it was. The man was George Hanson and the dog was Ryman setter Kathy's Farmboy Pete. George had just taken a position there with the U.S. Fish and Wildlife Service and was in the process of moving into a new apartment. This chance meeting was the beginning of a close association between George and a group of New England grouse hunters who became fans of the dogs. Our first setter was a gift from Bill—a puppy whose dam was straight out of the Appalachian Ryman lines.

When we first started, we bred to several dogs from various bloodlines, but breeding Holly to sons of Alder Run LeftiK produced setters closest to our ideals, and those breedings became the foundation of our kennel. This should not have been a surprise, as Walt and the other Appalachian breeders were serious grouse hunters who had proven their dogs on wild birds. Through cooperative breeding, this group of small breeders had maintained the lines in a way that normally only large breeders are able to do.

In addition to helping us as beginning breeders, Walt also gave us the opportunity during our visits to look through his Ryman pedigree collection, which piqued our interest in George Ryman's setters. We knew only a little about the history of the kennel at that time, and most "Rymans" we were familiar with were the bigger, linebred dogs derived from the later Calkins years. Seeing the many outside bloodlines Ryman used, along with studying his sales brochures, made us realize how different his dogs were from our concept of what a Ryman setter was. The many outcrosses and lack of linebreeding in the pedigrees were striking, and it was quite a shock to see what some of the setters in the old brochures looked like. Our naïve first reaction was that actual Rymans didn't look like Rymans! The photos in those brochures were of beautiful setters but they were short—coupled and athletic looking, many with conformation clearly influenced by field trial lines. The descriptions were of smaller sized setters than what we thought Rymans were supposed to be. Learning what the Rymans were really all about has been an intriguing study ever since.

Cliff and Lisa Weisse with October Sassy and October Mountain River.

Walt and George Bird Evans with Old Hemlock Jeb, Old Hemlock Dixie, and Old Hemlock Ruff.

My Ryman Setters

Old Hemlock Jeb

Jeb was my first English setter, whelped January 21, 1958, acquired as a pup from George Bird Evans, as described earlier. The entire litter was given Civil War names—like Dixie (the pup George kept for himself), Rebel, Jubal, etc. Old Hemlock Ruff sired this litter; the dam being Ryman's Blue Heather, who I took home along with her pup, as mentioned earlier in this writing.

Jeb developed into a rangy, long-coupled setter of about sixty pounds. According to my records, he was bred to Grouse Hill Dolly, who whelped eight pups in November, 1963. Dolly was owned by Harry Collander of Marietta, Ohio. George Hanson bred Jeb to his Alder Run Dawn, June 6, 1967. Dawn whelped 9 pups including my Seneca Grouse Tinker—my stud fee puppy. George had his usual kennel full and insisted I take two of the pups as a stud fee. I had previously been faced with the task of starting two identically aged pups at the same time and vowed I would never do so again! I selected an orange Belton (my first of this color) and another that reminded me of their dam. It wasn't very long before I found myself favoring the high-spirited orange Belton and knew immediately it was a grave error to take both pups.

I had learned that Bob Sumner sought a pup from this litter, so I offered the blue pup to him. Bob was still working for the State of West Virginia at that time, was scheduled to return to school to work on a graduate degree, but gladly accepted the pup gift. I should have known this to be a mistake when I heard about the school matter. The pup never left the end of a chain until I arranged for another ownership when it was two years old—which, unfortunately, turned out to be too late for this dog.

Jeb served me very well as a gun dog and was exposed to lots of birds at an early age; he handled grouse, quail, and woodcock equally. Jeb's major fault was jealousy. Try as we may, he never voluntarily honored the point of another dog. When this fault led to self-hunting, which he would do when another dog was braced with him, it was time for me to part ownership. This was before I owned an electronic training collar or knew of them being available, and I knew of no other humane way to deal with this problem. I placed Jeb with a young biologist who moved him to Missouri and gunned quail over him for the remainder of Jeb's life.

Alder Run Starr

Alder Run Starr, from the first litter of Appalachian Rymans, Ryman's Sky Joe x Ryman's Blue Heather.

Starr was a blue Belton female from my very first litter out of Ryman's Blue Heather, sired by Ryman's Sky Joe, and whelped on my birthday, December 15, in the year 1959. In my opinion, Starr's size and conformation was just about as perfect as a setter could be. She weighed 55 lbs., was short-coupled and had a very well conformed head. She was closely bonded to me and developed into a fine grouse dog. Starr learned to handle birds at an early age, at a time when birds—especially wild quail—were abundant. George Hanson acquired his Alder Run Dawn from this same litter, giving Burnell Davis an opportunity to carefully observe both dogs develop into good grouse dogs and confirming that we were on the right course producing typical Ryman setters. From what I had read and heard about setter characteristics as set forth by George Ryman, this litter met his criteria. I was delighted with the results and was on my way to maintaining the Ryman dogs.

Starr was not a big-ranging setter; I was able to hunt her in heavy cover with nothing more than a small sleigh bell. She was a comfortable dog to hunt in all types of cover. I had plenty of birds to enjoy with Starr and was not in any rush to breed her, but kept my eyes and ears open for a possible stud dog.

Sometime in the early 1960s I heard of a Ryman setter male owned by Stewart Thayer of Thomas, West Virginia. I followed this lead and found out that "Sarge," the setter I was seeking, had the run of the town of Thomas. Mr. Thayer, who owned and operated the "Sportsman's Club" in downtown Thomas, gave me a tour of the town looking for Sarge. We did not locate Sarge on the first attempt but found the large orange Belton setter another day. I then learned that Sarge routinely made the rounds of Thomas and, on one nightly tour, was taken in by the sheriff and locked in a jail cell to keep Sarge safe. The next morning the sheriff called Mr. Thayer who picked Sarge up at the jailhouse and took him home. Our breeding efforts were in vain; we could not get a mating.

On Starr's eighth birthday she was finally bred to Ryman's DeCoverly Pride, a handsome setter owned by Joe Lentz of Harrisville, West Virginia. She whelped five pups on February 17, 1968. I tried breeding her again in 1969 to Ryman's Shawnee Sage, owned by Joe Hvisdosa of Uniontown, PennysIvania, but Starr failed to conceive.

The scariest experience I had with a setter occurred during a winter grouse hunt with Joe Smith, just north of Elkins, on an old abandoned coal surface mine. We were working the top of a snow-covered ridge that had been encircled by the surface mine leaving a steep wall of approximately 50 to 60 feet high below us. The ridge top was reverting nicely to some excellent grouse habitat and we were getting some flushes. Joe took a shot at one of Starr's pointed grouse. We headed Starr in the direction of the bird's flight, feeling certain the bird had been hit. What I didn't realize was that we were heading Starr dangerously close to the edge of the high wall.

The next thing I knew Starr was missing! I could not hear her bell and my whistling brought no response. Finally, peering over the snow-covered edge very cautiously I saw Starr limping among the large rocks below. She responded to my frantic calling by looking up at me, but it was impossible for us to reach her. We found a break in the slope where the high wall was gradual enough to descend to the bench below, and joined up with the crippled setter.

I quickly examined Starr. She seemed to have no broken bones, but I could lift a front leg out almost 90 degrees—she had no use of that leg. We struggled to carry her out along the surface mine bench to our car.

We rushed Starr into Elkins and the only veterinarian available. The vet had an office in his home and placed Starr on his dining room table for the exam. I was annoyed, because he seemed to be more interested in a basketball game on television. He finally announced that the dog had no broken bones and there really wasn't anything he could do for her. Joe and I gathered up Starr once again and rushed her 55 miles north to the town of Clarksburg where I had a veterinarian friend standing by. Dr. Tom Hooton determined that all the muscle attached to her scapular had been torn free, but assured me that she would be all right. He wrapped the leg tightly to her body and said we should keep the leg immobile for several weeks.

Alder Run Starr was used as a model by artist Chuck Ripper for L.L. Bean's catalogs for the years 1971 & 2003.

I knew Starr would make a complete recovery when she cleared the bottom of a Dutch door to join me in the living room. Starr continued to be a wonderful companion and grouse dog. The only long-lasting result of the accident was a "hot" spot on her foot that remained hairless, requiring me to bandage it before each hunt—a small price to pay for such a dog!

Chuck Ripper, a West Virginia artist, was contracted by L.L. Bean to paint a cover for the 1971 issue of their hunting catalog. They wanted to illustrate a setter pointing a woodcock. Chuck was not familiar with English setters, so he joined me on an actual hunt to photograph a setter in action. We hunted the foothills of Cheat Mountain, where Starr successfully worked and pointed a single grouse, giving Chuck an ideal opportunity for shooting pictures. The cover painting turned out exceptionally well; both the woodcock and setter were accurately portrayed.

I recently toured the new Hunting and Fishing building at Freeport, Maine, and had an opportunity to see the marvelous display of catalog covers on the walls of this building. Feeling like a kid, I looked over my shoulder and felt like saying "that's my dog up there on the wall!"

Chuck Ripper's painting of Starr and a woodcock was also used again on the 2003 cover of Bean's fall hunting catalog.

Seneca Grouse Tinker

Seneca Grouse Tinker showing her glorious style.

Tinker was an outstanding setter and grouse dog—possibly my best grouse dog. Weighing in at 46 lbs., in good hunting shape—she convinced me that a setter this size is likely to excel in athletic ability. Her conformation was perfect. As to running, Tinker covered the ground thoroughly but fast. Burnell Davis described her as "too fast." By that he meant she covered the ground, satisfying herself that no bird was present and moved on to hunt new cover—thereby putting too much space between her and her handler. Yet Burnell preferred high spirited dogs like Tinker and I learned to like the same type of setter.

Tinker would retrieve but did not make a big fuss over the job. In her younger years, Tinker often failed to deliver the motionless bird to hand, but spit the bird out as she ran by. She did not want to waste any time on an unnecessary act. She once pointed a grouse while returning to me with a dead bird in her mouth—she spit the dead grouse out and focused on the one pointed.

Tinker came along before the age of beeper collars so I only ran her with a bell—the sheep-size bell that most of us used on our larger running dogs. I could hear quite well in Tinker's time, so usually just listened and walked in the direction where I last heard the bell. I sometimes had trouble locating her, but there were many occasions when I heard a slow staccato of bell rings that led me to her points. I wondered how she made that bell ring, because each time I found her motionless with a bird pinned.

One day, after the bell led me to my dog by just barely ringing, I quietly moved out of the thick cover and found her swaying from side to side; just enough to make the bell barely ring. As soon as Tinker saw me, she stiffened. Yes, the bird was there! I then realized that she was trying to help steer me to her when lost on point, but didn't want me to see her move.

Tinker had her own way of working grouse. She would not creep or slow down upon hitting the scent, but approached the bird at almost full throttle. Head held high, she quartered only if necessary, and stopped abruptly on the point. It was a real show to watch this setter work a bird. When a companion asked why Tinker didn't flush a grouse working it in this manner, I would say the bird was Tinkermerized!

Tinker was a product of George Hanson breeding his Alder Run Dawn (out of my first litter) to my Old Hemlock Jeb. She was whelped June 6, 1966, when George lived at Romney, West Virginia. Tinker is discussed elsewhere in this book,—and was the dog George Bird Evans desired to breed to Old Hemlock Briar.

My wife Ellie commissioned artist/biologist Thomas J. Allen to paint a portrait of Tinker from a slide of mine taken head-on following a long, hard grouse hunt, showing Tinker with bloodshot eyes. The result was a watercolor reproduced in the 1974 *West Virginia Hunting and Trapping* regulations. I did not get the original painting until the regulations were printed!

Tinker accompanied me on several gunning trips to the Bruce Peninsula in Ontario. She also hunted in Minnesota and Michigan along with states adjacent to West Virginia.

Seneca Grouse Tinker painting by noted artist/biologist Thomas J. Allen

Alder Run Heather

Alder Run Heather by Shadbush Ryman's Ruff and Seneca Grouse Tinker.

Orange Belton Heather was one of Tinker's pups sired by Shadbush Ryman's Ruff and whelped July 29, 1973. She was to be a stud fee pup, but instead I substituted Alder Run Jenny to be my stud fee obligation to Bob Sumner.

Jenny was out of a previous litter by Ruff and Tinker—another orange Belton who showed good promise as a gun dog for me until a particular sequence of events occurred. The reason for telling this story now is my sincere hope it might prevent someone from making the same mistake that I made.

Jenny was a youngster recently entering her first gunning season, and I was anxious to expose her to the woodcock migrating through Canaan Valley. I had not yet exposed her to any serious gunfire—nothing more than a blank pistol firing at the flush of a bird. To help the young dogs make that so important connection of a bird falling at the shot, I normally go it alone or with one other person who understands that I do not want a volley of gunfire at this point of a dog's experience. A group of close gunning friends and I were hunting out of a cabin in Canaan Valley. After spending about a day and a half sitting out a bad rainy period, everyone was anxious to pursue their favorite sporting activity. I decided the rain had eased off enough for me to take young Jenny out for some work and announced my plans to the rest of the party. Two other friends jumped up to go along and I couldn't say no. Although I preferred working the young dog by myself, they were just as anxious to get outdoors as I was.

I failed by not laying down some ground rules and permitted them to bring along guns. I did not carry a gun as a result, and decided to just handle Jenny. She worked the cover well and soon found and staunchly pointed a woodcock.

Instead of a single killing shot, which would have been ideal, there was a deafening volley of gunfire. This resulted in Jenny being gun-shy and blinking future birds—two very nasty man-caused faults—of which the former was new to me. I had dealt with the fault of blinking (bird-shyness) due to my association with Ryman's Blue Heather, as previously explained. I researched the subject of gun shyness and decided to use food removal system at the time of firing a shot—starting with a cap pistol and progressing to a shotgun. This method entails firing the gun as the dog starts to eat and removing the food pan promptly if the dog balks at the shot. I let Jenny eat a little more each day before firing the shot. This technique worked. Jenny gradually got over the gunfire and was allowed to finish her meal...but it was certainly hard on me.

Jenny was no longer gun-shy or a blinker, but something was seriously missing—spirit! She was no longer the enthusiastic, high spirited running setter she once was. Bob Sumner was anxious to use her in his breeding program, as she possessed the early Ryman bloodlines we all preferred. He gladly accepted Jenny to replace Heather as my stud fee.

Heather soon showed evidence of being a fine grouse and woodcock gun dog. She developed into a marvelous retriever, returning with dead or crippled grouse—sometimes under some very difficult circumstances. I recall more than one episode of a dead or crippled grouse falling into a deep, dark abyss and Heather coming out of the hole with a bird in her mouth. Heather was the only one of my setters to point a woodcock while she was in the process of returning with a bird she retrieved—and held everything while I photographed her. She was probably the easiest going setter I have owned, and was an absolute joy to be with. Everyone loved her.

During Heather's first gunning season, Jim Rawson and I were working his short-hair pointer, Cindy, and my Tinker in the hills of Lewis County, West Virginia. We left my pup,

Heather, in the car—hoping to get a late day opportunity to work her alone. It was a very trying hunt with both adult dogs competing terribly, and no grouse to be found. After several hours of this nonsense, those two dogs, who should have known better, flushed a large covey of quail. That was the last straw! We gathered up our wayward "kids" and headed for the car where Heather was anxiously awaiting our return—ever so hopeful of getting to hunt.

Up to this time, Heather had not had a productive grouse point. I planned to work her on the quail scattered by the other two delinquents.

Heather hunted well. She found and pointed a few of the quail and we managed to take three birds over her points. What really surprised us was the grouse Heather found and pointed that seemed to come from nowhere! We had six grouse flushes and Heather pointed two of them perfectly. Unfortunately, we missed each of these birds—perfectly! My journal indicated that both the grouse and quail were in dogwood cover, presumably eating the fruit of flowering dogwood which was extremely abundant that year. Heather made the day for us.

Heather accompanied me on many trips to Ontario, Minnesota, Michigan, and Florida and throughout our home covers. She died of a severe lung infection on August 24, 1984.

Harold Stillwell moving in on Heather's grouse point.

Heather with her last grouse retrieve.

Dawn's Shadbush Ted

Shadbush Ted with a mouthful of grouse.

Ted, also known as "Teddy," was bred by George Hanson and whelped June 3, 1977. A finer gun dog, coupled with his most unusual personality, could not be found. His breeding was the result of one quarter field trial bloodlines the likes of Beau Essig, Flight Commander, Glencrest Doctor, and Turnto—to name a few. The balance of his breeding was our own early Ryman bloodlines.

George had not done anything in the way of training—which was to my advantage. Ted bonded very easily and the socialization and obedience work came about very well. As I recall, the only part of his work that came slowly was staunchness. He was exposed to many wild birds but did not get solid on his points until a full two years of age. After breaking point, I would persistently set him up where he initially made the point, and made him stand in place for a while before releasing him. Of course, we also had "talks" about all the good-looking females that would come his way if he only did what he was bred to do. Once staunch, nothing short of a moving bird would cause Ted to budge a muscle.

Because of Ted's generally dark color, I had to hunt him with a wide blaze orange collar. I did this ever since the day I walked past without seeing him point his first grouse under a cluster of dark spruce trees. I felt terrible missing Ted's first productive grouse point. He was a comfortable dog to gun over, yet bold and aggressive.

Ted had a pleasant, but unusual, personality. He would eagerly leap into the vehicle prior to the hunt, but refused to load up afterwards. This required me to pick him up and physically load him. When I picked Ted up, he would go absolutely "dead dog" limp! This was a sight to behold—causing anyone watching the scene to break out laughing. One time, my son coaxed him to load up with a treat, but Ted never fell for that again!

One time I drove off to where Ted couldn't see me, parked, and walked back to see him curled up and whimpering right where I had left him. He simply did not want to leave the covers.

Another interesting trait was Ted's refusal to eat his daily biscuit or treat, so long as I petted and talked to him. He loved to hold a bird in his mouth and therefore was very easy to photograph in this manner. If there was a dead bird lying on the ground beside anyone when taking a break, Ted would surreptitiously slip up and "steal" the bird, just so he could walk around showing off. I called him "the thief." He was quite the character.

Ted had the conformation of a good Ryman setter—except his tail was held more like that of a field trial dog. As a young dog it was somewhere between 45 degrees and the "12 'o'clock tail." When he was on an unproductive point, or simply unsure of the scent, his sickle tail would curl back towards his head.

An accident occurred one day on a strip-mine bench in Lewis County, West Virginia. My crippled grouse had taken refuge in a pile of rocks at the base of the high wall. Ted, in frantic pursuit of the bird, jammed his head between a couple of these sharp-edged rocks and came out with the grouse in his mouth; however, his eye was bleeding profusely. Ted delivered the grouse to me in usual fashion but all I could see was the blood pouring from his eye. I used my shooting glove to apply pressure and get the bleeding under control. Fearful that the bleeding would start again, I walked him at heel all the way to my vehicle. I knew that I wouldn't get back to Elkins before 10:00 pm, so called my wife to make arrangements for a veterinarian to be on standby. Dr. G. J. Crissman met me at the clinic, took one look at the gash in a corner of Ted's eye and announced, "This is going to be a real challenge." Dr. Crissman did a fine job of surgery and Ted was no worse for the wear.

Another time Ted just quit hunting, ran to me, put his front feet on my chest and looked directly at my face. It was then I saw a stick—and I mean a stick—maybe ¼ inch in diameter and 3 inches long, protruding from his eye. I promptly pulled it out and he returned to his job of hunting.

During his prime, Ted was bred to a lot of related bitches and produced a lot of good gundogs, however some litters met with a higher than normal degree of mortality.

As mentioned previously, Ted and Heather made the best brace of gun dogs I ever ran—always with the best of manners and not a hair of jealousy between them.

One fine January 1985 day, I was hunting some of the old Lewis County, West Virginia, mined areas, squeezing in a hunt between some major snowstorms. The south slopes were just beginning to open up, affording some welcome bare ground and I took advantage of this rare winter opportunity by working three of my setters—Ted, Tara, and Gypsy. The "girls" were working well and I took one grouse over Tara's point with Gypsy backing. Tara backed Gypsy on another grouse, which did not afford a shooting opportunity. Ted pointed below a gas well road. I stepped off the road, promptly fell on my rear and slid down the road bank, making a lot of noise as I fell. This caused Ted to turn his head, looking at me as if to say, "What the hell are you doing now?" I never saw the grouse.

Dawn's Shadbush Ted. *Photo by Lefty Kreh*

Alder Run Tara

Alder Run Tara.

Chapter 9

A daughter of Heather and Ted, Tara was a 47 to 50 lb. tricolor, line bred to our early Ryman bloodlines. She was whelped July 6, 1981. Her conformation, size, and gait were just perfect, as far as I was concerned. She ran with a straight back and glided along—I called it "fluid drive," and in that respect was very similar to Ryman's Blue Heather. She was such a joy to watch running, and turned into a fine, dependable, gun dog on grouse and woodcock...except, as a young dog, when she competed with her brace mate.

Tara's first grouse was taken on Ontario's Bruce Peninsula, where for several years I worked my dogs in October for early season training and gunning wild birds. A dog's first grouse kill is always remarkable and Tara's was especially so. She pointed in a tried and true aspen cover, with the bird pinned close between us. As the grouse climbed before me, I connected with it squarely. The bird dropped directly into my left hand, bounced off, and fell to the ground. I almost caught it in hand! My journal records: "I was thrilled—lots of pictures taken of the event." Alder Run Gypsy also had her first grouse taken in this same Ontario aspen cover one year later.

Grouse numbers on the Bruce were consistently good, along with very good woodcock numbers, overly generous limits, and many snipe. By the time I returned to the home covers in West Virginia, the dogs were in great shape for the rest of the fall seasons. All this bird exposure, coupled with the good grouse numbers we had in home covers through the eighties, contributed to the fine gun dogs I had. I considered myself to be overly blessed with having four fine grouse dogs in my kennel at the same time! Four is the maximum number of personal gun dogs or breeders that I have allowed in my kennel. I did this to be fair to the dogs, assuring that I would give each setter the attention they deserve and time spent in the covers. As I grew older, I found that two setters were plenty of dog power for me!

I would be remiss if I did not at least mention my other setters so, in the interest of not belaboring this chapter, there was: Alder Run LeftiK, Alder Run Jinjer, Shadbush Lancelot, and Alder Run Jennie, who, at over 13 years, was still finding and pointing birds. My latest setter is October Alder Run Dolly who is as near a perfect grouse and woodcock gun dog as they come and highly intelligent.

Alder Run Tara bringing home the grouse.

Alder Run Gypsy

Chapter 9

Alder Run LeftiK

Alder Run Jinjer

Chapter 9

Shadbush Lancelot

Alder Run Jennie

PART V
GROUSE HUNTING IN THE APPALACHAIN MOUNTAINS

The places where grouse live are called "covers" or "coverts—but by any name, they are a fool's paradise...and we continually prove that by being so happy when we're in them.

—That's Ruff
...by George King

Walt shooting over Alder Run Heather in a typical Appalachian hawthorn cover. *Photo by Lefty Kreh.*

Walt Saling about to take a grouse over a point by Alder Run Heather. Notice Walt's successful approach from the side and where he can clearly see the flush from the grapevines shown on the bank below the bench where he is standing.

In Pursuit of the "Woods Pheasant"

This discussion of grouse hunting applies to the southern Appalachians—and particularly to the mountains and hills of West Virginia. The Mountain State is blessed with diverse flora due to its geographic location and its elevation variances, ranging from 240 feet above sea level at the Harpers Ferry National Monument to over 4,800 feet at Spruce Knob.

As a result, grouse cover in the hardwoods of the central and western counties will be different from that in the northern hardwoods of the high mountains—or covers in the oak-pine forest type of the Ridge and Valley in the eastern panhandle.

The central and western hills, while not so high, are steep-sided with numerous natural benches that are a distinct benefit to the grouse hunter. A sidehill will normally have two or more of these benches, depending on the height of the hill, making it convenient for a hunting party—with each hunter following a bench. One caveat though: I have had an occasional problem with dogs being confused by following the wrong bench while attempting to locate me. Windy conditions can make this more of a problem.

Moist north and east slopes are rich in greens on the forest floor. These greens are a preferred food for grouse year-round. Grapevines are found in the deep, rich soils of these central hardwood coves. Some important shrubs and vines that provide food for grouse are grapes, flowering dogwood, greenbrier, panicled or grey dogwood in the northern panhandle counties, serviceberry, crabapple, and bittersweet. Some other preferred foods are spicebush, poison ivy, sumac, and black haw.

The narrow razor-backed ridges of southwestern West Virginia counties have a very similar central hardwood forest type, but are without natural benches. Surface mine benches provide grouse hunter access in this otherwise very steep terrain. Grouse populations in these southwestern counties are more stable than any other region of the state. This is due to a number of factors, among them being a milder climate, deep fertile soils, and importantly, because of the milder climate, more consistent mast crops. Southeastern counties are more of a gentle topography with similar cove hardwoods, turning into the oak-pine type of the Ridge and Valley as we progress easterly.

In the higher mountains, northern hardwoods occur mostly in a zone from 3,000 feet to over 4,000 feet in elevation. The major components are sugar maple, beech, and yellow birch. Black cherry is another component of northern hardwoods of interest to the grouse hunter. The major conifers (evergreens) are red spruce, hemlock, and white pine. Expansive rhododendron thickets are common at these high elevations and, along with the conifers, serve grouse by furnishing escape and energy conservation covers.

The shrubs of interest to the grouse hunter in the northern hardwood type include hawthorn, red elderberry, and hobble-bush, a few species of deciduous holly, wild raisin, witch-hazel, and serviceberry. Hawthorn is the most important of these shrubs, because of its habit of forming pure dense stands where allowed to do so, and its reliable production of food for grouse. Woodcock commonly rest and probe for food in hawthorn stands where the stem density is heavy and the slopes have no more than 3% gradient and are grazed by cattle to keep grasses and other plants close to the ground.

East of the Allegheny Front, in the eastern panhandle of West Virginia, the forests are described as oak and oak-pine and, being in a rain shadow of the Allegheny Front, the soils are dry. Mountain laurel is a common understory plant that furnishes grouse cover and, when acorns are scarce and the ground is covered with snow, grouse will eat mountain laurel leaves and buds. Flowering dogwood and witch-hazel are common shrubs of interest to the grouse hunter. Also of interest is scrub oak, which grows on the dry soils of this region commonly following heavy cutting or repeated fires.

As in other forest types, moist soils of the bottoms and north and east slopes grow important green plants, highly productive grape tangles and greenbrier thickets—all good components of grouse habitat.

Mostly due to heavy foliage conditions, serious grouse hunting doesn't traditionally take place until sometime in December. This applies to much of West Virginia's lowlands. Hunting in the mountains, where foliage is much lighter at the high elevations, typically takes place with the opening of grouse and woodcock seasons.

My Ryman setter and grouse hunting mentor, Burnell Davis, looked forward to the early snows. Burnell claimed they would cause grouse to bunch up in their winter habitat, which were usually greenbrier thickets where they find both food and shelter. This has proven true over the years and is especially helpful in these Appalachian Mountains because the early snows do not last long due to the warm ground, allowing us to hunt on snow free ground again.

The woodlands of October and November have a special charm for me, one that cannot be found at any other time of year. The same appeal northern states have for hunting grouse in October; apply to the high mountains of West Virginia. However, I feel, given favorable weather conditions in January and February, when scenting conditions are at their best, the dog work and quality of grouse hunting are superior. The exception would be when wind is from the south, resulting in poor scent conditions that can adversely affect the quality of dog work. I also believe that grouse hold for a dog much better during these late season months.

I prefer hunting on bare ground, feeling the only benefit snow can add to the enjoyment of a hunt is that it reveals a story that can only be speculated without the snow. I have seen tracks of unseen and unheard grouse that positioned themselves on an elevated rock or log, facing in the direction of my approaching dogs, and then simply left the scene without our knowledge. Without the snow to tell the story, I might get a point without a flush as the only indication of the birds' presence.

The Appalachian grouse hunter can expect to find woodcock in late February. These are males returning from their wintering place and performing courtship activities as they migrate to their breeding grounds. I commonly find woodcock here after February 20—sometimes a

Alder Run Jinjer pointing grouse in the late autumn woods.

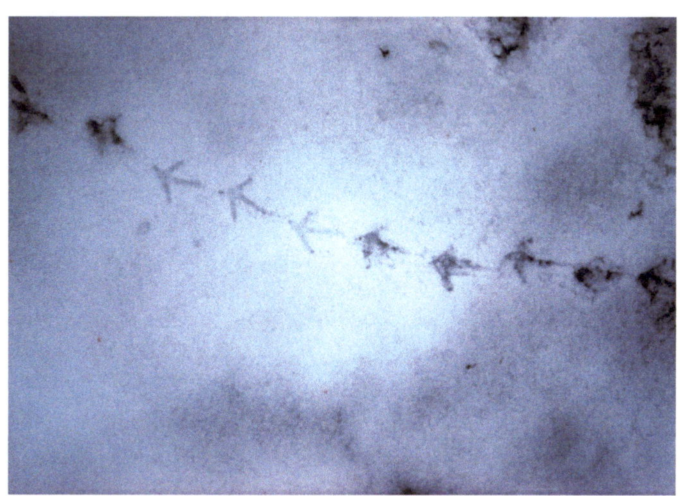

week earlier, depending on the weather. I enjoy the added dog work while hunting grouse—adding a "catch and release" form of hunting (woodcock season is closed this time of year) and reminding me of the forthcoming breeding and nesting seasons. I also like to work my setters on returning woodcock after grouse season, especially when there is some dog training to be done. However, I strongly believe in keeping my dogs out of the woods after the end of March. This, for the most part, prevents conflicts with nesting birds and minimizes the harassment of wild birds—they get enough of this from their natural predators.

I have centered this discussion on hunting grouse with dogs, neglecting to address hunting without a canine companion. The reason being this writing is primarily about Ryman setters, and of course, my interest in hunting grouse with these setters. I believe that if someone is in the woods with the primary purpose to *kill* grouse, they will probably be better off without a pointing dog. However in my opinion, that person will be missing a great deal! I believe 75% of my enjoyment of a grouse hunt is centered on the dog and its work—the balance of my pleasure afield is seeing where the grouse lives. Should the reader be interested in finding grouse without the aid of a dog, there is plenty of helpful literature available.

Be aware, however, I am not belittling hunting grouse without a dog. Thinking back over the years of grouse hunting—I have learned a lot about grouse from the different dogs I have hunted. The dogs have shown me much about the bird we were seeking. I can imagine that a hunter pursuing the sport without the help of a dog would have to learn by trial and error from the grouse he is hunting. A lot can be said for the lone hunter seeking grouse and not having the distraction of watching a dog, or the dog disturbing natural movement of birds and animals in the course of the hunt.

I have recently been introduced to one method of winter grouse hunting without the use of dogs. A friend calls his method of dog-less grouse hunting "hunting snow holes." He hunts for places where grouse have snow roosted, leaving depressions on the surface, attracting him to investigate and flush the roosting grouse. This friend desires at least 12 inches of the white stuff for successful "snow hole" hunting, and pursues his favorite way of grouse hunting on snowshoes.

Grouse hunters are pretty much of a breed, whether they hunt the Appalachians, northeast, or Midwest. However they may have language difficulties. By this I mean they do not all talk the same and communication between them may sometimes be difficult. This problem can occur locally, regionally or even between states.

Some grouse hunters play the numbers game—how many birds killed on a hunt, season, or whatever, in relating the enjoyment he or she got out of a hunt or season. If a dog man is doing the talking, he will relate to other hunters in terms of the number of points during a day's hunt. This will work if the hunter fills out the story with details—like how many flushes, hours spent hunting, and anything else that will give the person he is talking to a total mental picture of the hunt. Different hunters define their measure of success or contentment in different ways.

Walt Saling after a good day in the covers. Shown also are (L to R): Alder Run Heather, Shadbush Ted, Grouse Woods Brandy and Cider.

Chapter 10

I believe that the best way to describe a hunt—whether I'm talking to another hunter or filling out a survey form—is to talk in terms of flushes per hour of actual hunting time. Sure, I'm keeping track of my dog's productive points for the sake of my journal, but this is often something no one else cares about and besides, it could be taken as bragging! Flushes per hour reveal the day's success in terms of bird numbers. In telling about a day's hunt, it isn't necessary to give any additional information unless asked for more. Maybe I got this way because of my career as a wildlife biologist. I remembered talking with the late noted woodcock biologist William Goudy, who would relate his hunting experiences in terms of flushes per hour—and I could quickly get a feeling for the kind of day he was talking about or in the case of woodcock, what I might expect of the flights if I got into the covers.

We really get to know each other by spending time together in the grouse woods. George King, the author of *That's Ruff,* (Concord House Publishing, 2010) related the following story he received from Burnell Davis of Pennsboro, West Virginia.

> It seems that a credit man from a bank or finance company was checking on the reputation of a local resident who had applied for a loan. In doing so, he stopped at the farm next door to inquire about this man and the following conversation took place:
>
> "Say, do you know Sam Johnson from the next farm?"
> "Yep."
> "How long has he lived here."
> "Ever since I been here."
> "How long is that?"
> "Bout forty years."
> "Well, what kind of fellow is he?"
> "Don't really know."
> "I mean, is he a pretty honest sort of man?"
> "Don't really know."
> "Well, what *do* you know about him?"
> "Not much."
> "Good Heavens, man! You've lived next to him for forty years! You must know *something* about him!"
> "Well, Yeah, I know he ain't a grouse hunter."

There is one more item that would be an appropriate quote here from George King's book *That's Ruff:*

> When a man continually talks about how many birds he's killed, instead of flushes, misses, and unusual experiences, it's a safe bet he has a .410 brain and a 12 gauge ego.

Donna Lesser watering Alder Run LeftiK and Jinjer

Lefty Kreh proudly showing his "trophy" – a grouse taken over Ted's point. Good friend and hunting partner, Raleigh Boaze is in the background.

L. to R.: Lefty Kreh, Raleigh Boaze, and Ed Dentry, with Heather and Ted after a day hunting grouse in the salad bowls.

Hunting the Salad Bowls

We were hunting a narrow strip of woods between open pasture and an old strip-mine above, taking advantage of a late season opportunity to hunt on snow-free ground. The stream bottom below us was abandoned farmland—all in all, ideal grouse habitat. The strip of woods was broken with small drainages containing "salad bowls"—the objects of our afternoon hunt.

As we dropped into the first drain, my tricolor setter, Ted, began acting birdy. Pointing, then breaking, pointing, and moving again—we knew by his actions that Ted had a grouse running ahead through a salad bowl. The bird flushed wildly—as they will often do in open woods, with no dense cover to make them feel secure. Soon Ted's orange Belton bracemate Heather, another Ryman setter, pinned a grouse above yet another salad bowl. This bird escaped through the only patch of cover around, without a shot being fired.

This was a February hunt with Lefty Kreh, Ed Dentry, and Raleigh Boaze in the West Virginia hill country. I don't usually hunt with this many people, but these are very special friends gathered for a special occasion. Lefty is a world renowned flyfisher, writer, photographer, and entertainer, yet few know him as a bird hunter. He has thoroughly enjoyed grouse and woodcock gunning, and the same well-developed hand and eye coordination of a superb fly caster enables him to be an excellent hand with the scattergun. No hunter shows greater enthusiasm behind a good working dog.

As we neared another salad bowl, a grouse whirled away unscathed. Excitedly, Lefty shouted Ed's way: "What'd I tell you—these salad bowls are dynamite."

Salad bowls are spring seeps or drain areas on north and east slopes of the Appalachian Mountains that quickly thaw winter snows because of the warm temperature of emerging ground water. Even during the rigors of winter, they produce lush green herbaceous vegetation. Salad areas are located on deep, fertile soils—moist, because they are on north and east-facing slopes. These areas attract grouse during the winter months and therefore are of great interest to grouse hunters and dog trainers. The moist, protected aspects of salad bowls produce lush small green-leaved plants that are groceries for grouse—Christmas and grape ferns, ragwort, chickweed, clover, cinquefoil, and others. Wild grape vines are often found in or near the salad bowls. They provide low, dense covers that make grouse feel secure and furnish another food source during winter. Grouse are not apt to run so much from pointing dogs in areas of heavy grape cover on the ground. Salad bowls with grape tangles or thick young tree growth are even more attractive to the winter grouse hunter.

Grouse are opportunistic in their feeding habits and will eat what is available in the way of leaves, fruits, and buds of forest plants. Their menu includes a very large number of herbaceous and woody plants. This bird's range of distribution covers more area of the North American continent than any other non-migratory game bird. Appalachian grouse do not eat the same foods as grouse in the northern Lake States for the very reason that Appalachian vegetation is much more diverse than in the northern states. More diverse vegetation means a greater variety of available food including a greater number of green plants added to the grouse grocery list.

Green plants are the one constant in the adult bird's diet throughout the year. Grouse eat this salad whenever available. Thus the reason why salad bowls, as we like to call them, are so attractive to grouse. They prefer this gourmet food to their usual winter diet—the buds of woody plants.

In his classic work, *The Ruffed Grouse: Its Life Story, Ecology, and Management,* Frank C. Edminster suggests that leaves of plants are the most staple food for grouse in the northeastern states. In another study of early winter game foods from 263 bird crops collected in southwest Pennsylvania and northern West Virginia, the authors found that six of the eight foods most often found in the crops were ferns or the leaves of green plants. The common greens reported taken by grouse in this study were crowfoot, Christmas fern, chickweed, and goldenrod/aster.

Do not get the idea that grouse management only focuses on herbaceous plants as food for these birds. Good forest management for grouse should include the provision of food in the form of mast (fruits) such as acorns and beechnuts, along with cover (young forest growth) in close proximity, as well as greens. In the oak forests of the Appalachians, this can be done by the use of clearcutting, shelterwood, two-age, or group selection cutting. Preferred green foods, such as clover and birdsfoot trefoil can be planted on log roads.

This should be no revelation to an experienced Appalachian Mountain grouse hunter who has gunned the wild grape tangles on north and east slopes—or where strip-mine high walls pinch off in moist drains, leaving salad bowls accessible to the gunner and his canine companion. Sooner or later the hunter should realize that the birds he found were after something in particular—if he bothered to examine crop contents of the birds he had taken. The veteran grouse hunter plans the hunt carefully so he and his dog will be in favored feeding areas, such as salad bowls, during the magic feeding hours of late afternoon.

One way to plan a hunt in unfamiliar territory is with the aid of topographic maps. Likely areas for salad bowls can be located in advance by examining north and east slopes on the map and then field checking these areas during the hunt. I enjoy exploring new covers in this manner even if nothing is found. No one is more optimistic than a grouse hunter!

Fly fishers seeking trout find it useful to learn what their quarry was eating, in order to match the hatch. While this is not as critical when hunting less selective grouse, it does help the gunner to locate birds. The study of grouse food habits adds to a hunter's knowledge of the bird's life cycle and habits. It certainly adds another dimension to the hunt—just as matching the hatch or fly tying does for the fly fisherman.

Some years ago my gunning partner Buck and I were working a large hawthorn cover in West Virginia's high country. There was an abundance of hawthorn fruit that year and practically nothing else for grouse to eat in the way of early season fruits and hard mast. Finding only woodcock, we assumed there weren't any grouse to be had. As the day wore on, we started to find a few grouse in the "thorn apples," but the birds were flushing wildly in the open hawthorn understory. My setter Jinjer took a wide swing and covered the width of this large hawthorn cover before circling to approach us head on. She froze in high style—pinning two grouse between her and us. Both grouse exploded, one quartering back to my left, offering an easy chance to drop the bird in front of Jinjer, who was quickly on it for the retrieve. Buck and I examined the young rooster's crop, expecting to find it full of thorn apples. There were lots of hawthorn fruit—and many off-white, pieces of soft plant material. Neither of us could identify this material, so I checked with a local botanist who identified them as "Beechdrops," a parasitic plant that only grows on the roots of American beech trees. Mystery solved; we were not finding grouse in the "thorns" earlier in the day, because the birds had been in a nearby beech woods prior to feeding in the hawthorns!

If plant identification is not your cup of tea, try comparing the shapes of leaves found in grouse crops to the plants found in your covers. Studying the food habits of the bird you hunt will result in a greater understanding and appreciation of the components of good grouse habitat. It also adds another facet of interest to a great sport.

A great variety of green plants constitute the winter's diet of grouse. This single bird's crop contents came from Greenbrier County, West Virginia.

Below is a list of plants commonly found in the fall and winter crops of ruffed grouse.[1] These plant names have been taken from a study of grouse foods in the southern Appalachian Mountains, in addition to my own examinations of winter grouse crops over the years.

COMMON NAME	GENUS
Crowfoot	Ranunculus
Cinquefoil	Potentilla
Greenbrier	Smilax
Bedstraw	Galium
Christmas fern	Polystichum
Alumroot	Heuchera
Common chickweed	Stellaria
Aster	Aster
Grapefern	Botrychium
Wild strawberry	Fragaria
Golden ragwort	Senecio
Mountain Laurel	Kalmia

Plant varieties like these make salad bowls a drawing card for grouse. Despite unseasonably high temperatures, poor scent conditions, and unfavorable winds, in two days of hunting with Lefty, Ed, and Raleigh, we recorded 47 grouse flushes, mostly from salad bowls. Pouring over topographic maps and field checking the north and east facing slopes had paid good dividends. The hunters and setters were happy. I'd recommend checking out salad bowls for your late season hunts.

Green leaves, high in protein, make up a large part of an Appalachian ruffed grouse diet.

Ted takes a well-deserved break to cool off in a seep draining a productive salad bowl area.

Kurt Oelmann with Black Satan JoJo, out of Queen's Widmont JoJo X Misty Meadows Blossom.

Grouse in the Grape Tangles

Satan Comes to Bogsucker Creek

Kurt Oelmann had a Ryman setter named Satan; Black Satan JOJO, to be exact. This dog was bred by our mutual friend, George Hanson, and was Kurt's pride and joy. He wanted a pup out of Satan very badly. Badly enough to leave Satan with a breeder for a period of time, hoping that he would sire a litter of pups. As far as Kurt knew, he did not succeed.

Looking for a good Ryman stud dog to breed one of my bitches, I arranged for a get together with Kurt and Satan. I wanted to see how Satan hunted and hopefully watch him work wild birds. I knew of a cover on Bogsucker Creek; there was a good mix of alder and other shrubs and young hardwoods, making up a nice riparian habitat along the margin. I had found woodcock, along with an occasional grouse, in this cover. There would be enough dense cover mixed with openings to evaluate Satan's work.

Satan hit the cover hard and worked it thoroughly, using the wind to his advantage, demonstrating his ability as an experienced grouse dog. Not finding a bird in the first twenty minutes of hunting caused Satan to move out beyond Kurt's comfort range. Kurt did not have a whistle. Instead, he called the dog repeatedly. "Come Satan—Satan Come" he called, in an effort to turn the dog back to us.

Then I looked to my right, facing a cemetery at the top of the slope, across Bogsucker Creek from where we stood. There was a tent set up with people under the canopy assembled around a gravesite. Other people were standing outside the canopy. It suddenly occurred to me that a funeral was in progress. My thoughts were broken again as Kurt cried out: "Come Satan—Satan Come."

I knew the funeral proceeding was in earshot of Kurt's hailing to Satan. I knew I had to interrupt Kurt's calling Satan before we caused the deceased to go in the wrong direction! We moved on!

Delayed Retrieves

In my years of grouse hunting, I have realized that sometimes it takes a little longer than expected to retrieve a downed bird.

I was working two setters, my Tara and Gypsy, in some cutover woods in the upper Tygart River Valley. This was a bare ground, winter hunt in a year when beech mast was extremely abundant. Can you imagine being able to pick up beechnuts off the forest floor in February! A rare feat at this time of year since beechnuts are a favorite food of all forest dwellers. This cover was a bit past prime in terms of grouse habitat and had a lot of producing beech trees throughout.

My two girls were working well and I was fortunate to pick up two grouse on this late afternoon hunt before Gypsy pointed a brace of birds. My timing must have been as good as it gets, because each bird fell at my shots. Gypsy had no difficulty with the retrieve of one grouse and delivered the bird promptly. The other downed bird however, could not be located by either of the two setters in spite of a diligent search. Realizing the lost bird represented the last grouse of my four bird daily limit, I encouraged the dogs to bee-line it towards our vehicle—we had done enough damage for one day.

The next legal time afield was two days away, and while I had no interest in hunting this cover so soon again, I wanted to make another attempt at finding the lost grouse. I felt certain it was down and had not reflushed. The next hunting day was a Monday and I decided to use two different setters to hopefully locate the downed grouse. I directed LeftiK and Jinjer to the general area where the bird had fallen. It didn't take LeftiK very long to locate, point, and retrieve the wing-tipped, but otherwise healthy grouse within 100 yards of where I thought it had dropped. The grouse had been feeding when found, leaving a scent trail that aided LeftiK in locating this bird, thereby filling out my limit of two days previous.

Years back Jim Rawson and I were hunting some of the original clearcuts done on the Monongahela National Forest in northern Greenbrier County. We had brought a bird down over one of Alder Run Starr's points. Even though both Starr and Jim's "Cindy," a German shorthair pointer, were both accomplished dead-bird finders and retrievers, we could not locate our downed grouse. One week later—to the day—we were hunting the same area, when Starr went on point. Fully expecting a flush, I walked in and saw the grouse calmly walking away from the point with an obvious broken wing. Starr was sent in for the retrieve, which she did effectively. Jim took this bird home and reported seven number 8 pellet strikes in the body of the grouse. The bird's crop was half full of freshly eaten greens.

Another week-long delayed retrieve occurred on Breathed Mountain—now part of the Dolly Sods Wilderness. I was guiding a party of Long Island friends on the margins of a large bog area. This was a favorite grouse cover, because I could take a break to pick and eat wild cranberries as a bonus. Tinker pointed in a stunted stand of spruce. It was a snap shot but I could see the bird fall through the spruce limbs. Tinker could not find the bird in the muskeg that covered the ground under that thick spruce. One week later, while hunting a different section of this vast area, I swung by the same clump of spruce and Tinker found and delivered my bird to hand—with a crop full of fresh cranberries; an added bonus!

What Makes a Double?

Most discussions on the subject of doubles do not consider it a true double unless both birds take flight at the same time. To me a double on any bird consists of a situation where I have two birds on the ground, or on the water, at the same time. A two for one double, when two birds fall at a single shot, can easily happen with geese, ducks, and doves, but rarely occurs on grouse or woodcock.

The finest double shooting I ever witnessed was achieved by my cousin and great friend, Bill Donaldson. We were hunting an alder cover along the Blackwater River in Canaan Valley. Bill's German shorthair pointed and two snipe were in the air followed by two reports from Bill's Daley double. Both snipe fell to the ground as clean kills. The work could not have

L to R: Alder Run LeftiK, Alder Run Gypsy, and Alder Run Tara after taking 3 grouse and failing to retrieve the 4th bird of that day's limit.

been done in a cleaner manner. Besides that, shooting in alders has never been an easy matter for me—especially on a bird with the erratic flight of a snipe.

My first grouse double was in alders along the Blackwater River on land that is now a part of the Canaan Valley State Park—where hunting is no longer permitted. My setter Starr had the point. I dropped one grouse on my side of the river with the second grouse falling in the river. Starr saw the bird hit the water and promptly dove in for the retrieve. She picked up the grouse, but never turned back. Instead, she swam to the far bank, got out of the water still holding onto the bird, turned to face me and proceeded to eat the grouse, while I kept yelling the command "Fetch"—which was totally ignored! Starr was young at the time and, I suppose, thought she was deserving of this meal after a wet, hard hunt. Starr never attempted to eat another bird.

Another double was made high atop Breathed Mountain when grouse were bunched up under hawthorn trees with nothing but open space around a single hawthorn or small clump. In some years it was common to find groups of grouse under such trees feasting on thornapples—the fruit of the hawthorn. When found under these conditions, with a dog pointing, it was no great feat to take a bird with each barrel.

My favorite double of all is the father/son double. To qualify as such, the birds must be pointed and the father and son or daughter, each taking a bird. This has happened with my son, Hunter, and I twice. The first time it occurred, we were hunting the upper Tygart Valley in West Virginia's Randolph County. I had just gotten back from a trip to northern Minnesota where, in good habitat, we could average 10 grouse flushes per hour. The habitat was 8-12 year-old aspen with a hazelnut shrub understory. It was just about a peak population year in Minnesota. Back to West Virginia, Hunter and I were gunning over Tinker and had flushed forty-five grouse in 4 ½ hours of effort—the same flush rate I experienced in Minnesota! I should point out that I do not make a practice of following up a grouse after the first flush. Of course, this day there wasn't a need for that anyway. We did have a few groups of birds under Tinker's points that day and, from one of these points, each of us took a grouse simultaneously.

Another father/son double occurred a couple years later on Glade Run of the Blackwater River in Canaan Valley. Tinker had two grouse under point in a woods edge. We fired simultaneously without knowledge of the other shooting, and each of us took a bird. Neither of us was even cognizant of another bird being in the air while concentrating on our own bird.

An early goal in my shooting life was to make a true grouse/woodcock double—that is to take a grouse and woodcock with each flushing simultaneously. I never did accomplish this goal. However, my shooting journal of November 1, 1980, indicates that while hunting my young tricolor setter Ted in a great Randolph County hawthorn cover "I had a dead woodcock and grouse on the ground at the same time—but not a true double!" Had that event occurred later in my shooting life, it would most certainly have been considered a true grouse/woodcock double!

On still another occasion, my setter Ted and a shooting partner had just entered a cover when two grouse came flying past me, one following the other, and each fell to my shots. Ted promptly went to the birds, lying only a few feet apart. He stood between them looking at each grouse, one lying still and the other flopping its wings, then proceeded to the bird in motion and promptly delivered it to me. I was extremely proud of Ted at this point, fetching the bird that still had mobility rather than the one lying motionless. But immediately after

Ted retrieving a grouse to Walt. *Photo by Lefty Kreh.*

that retrieve, Ted went on hunting, forgetting all about the second grouse. I then realized that Ted had a weakness—he couldn't count!

Ghost Grouse

Burton Spiller wrote about coming upon a large group of grouse which disappeared from his cover after the initial flush, never to be located again. Such an event happened to me. I was hunting in some of Barbour County's oak-hickory woods fragmented by small fields, with my setter Starr. We were approaching a group of young white oaks of mast-bearing age, with lots of acorns on the ground. As we entered these woods, the ground erupted with grouse. I don't remember Starr even going on point. I know there must have been at least 20 birds flushing, maybe more. They didn't all flush simultaneously, of course, but there were so many of them that all I could do was estimate numbers.

I was not close enough to take a shot—and had I been close enough; I was too awestruck to take a shot! And naturally, young Starr went wild, running hard with excitement and flushing the birds that might otherwise have held. Both of us were panting with excitement, and sat down to cool off for 15 minutes or so. My plan was to let the grouse settle down and move about, leaving some scent trails. It wasn't very long after we started hunting again that Starr pointed a single grouse, which fell to my shot and she retrieved. With plenty of daylight left, this evening was going to be one of the best ever; I had thoughts of grouse scattered all over the landscape! Starr and I kept working the cover, moving in a concentric pattern, working farther and farther from the initial flush site—but we never found another grouse! Nor did we ever see any indication that a grouse had been nearby! I began to wonder if I really did see that large number of birds. Perhaps it was a figment of my imagination?

An Exceptional Piece of Dog Work

Hunter and I, along with my orange Belton setter Tinker, were hunting a tributary of the Blackwater River in Canaan Valley. We encountered a good number of woodcock, a few grouse, and noticed an abundance of "whitewash" splashing in the open understory of St Johns Wort vegetation. The splashing appeared to be fresh woodcock sign, and Tinker was working this sign. We soon discovered that it wasn't woodcock sign at all. A flight of Common snipe were running ahead of Tinker's points, due to the open ground beneath the St Johns Wort, and flushing wildly ahead. We did not get a shot at a snipe, but the observation was one of interest. Snipe, to me have their own mystique, which in many ways are similar to woodcock. I love to hear the flushed snipe's call, sounding much like the word "scaipe" and they are a lot of fun to shoot at!

Tinker pointed a woodcock close to the riverbank, which flushed and flew across the river, falling at our shots on the far side in a heavy alder thicket. The stream, dammed up by beavers, was too wide and deep for our fording and Tinker had not marked the falling bird. With a good bit of encouragement, I offered the command "dead bird, fetch" Tinker dove in and swam to the far bank, disappearing into the alders.

After what seemed like a long period of time, Tinker appeared at the far bank with a dead woodcock in her mouth. Much to my surprise, she laid the bird down and went back into the alders. Her bell went silent and we looked at each other as if to say "ok, what do we do now?" After waiting a few minutes for something to happen, I picked up a large stick and flung it as hard as I could into those alders on the far side of the stream. When it landed, a grouse flushed. After this, Tinker appeared at the bank once again. Now she picked up the dead woodcock and swam across to deliver the bird to us. Apparently she had encountered the grouse while searching for the downed woodcock, and possessed the savvy to deliver the dead woodcock to the bank within our sight, then returned to point the grouse previously found. I have not seen this sort of dog work duplicated.

Muzzleloader Grouse

When the woods seem devoid of grouse, I have heard hunters claim that the birds must have all retreated to woodchuck dens. I have actually witnessed crippled grouse take refuge in groundhog dens or similar holes between rocks, but never dreamed a healthy bird would do so.

One winter day, while hunting a reclaimed area where coal had previously been surface-mined, my orange Belton setter Jinjer went on a picture-perfect point in a very open area. While approaching, I couldn't help but think: this was no place for a grouse! It was the poorest habitat situation I could imagine. The ground was covered with a dense mat of tall fescue grass, while the over story was almost non-existent—just a few widely scattered small black locust trees—nothing more!

Jinjer never moved a hair as I approached. I could not imagine this was a grouse and wondered just what she was pointing. Jinjer normally pointed only feathered critters. I was standing close to her when I saw the head of a grouse appear above the grass mat 10 to 15 yards ahead. The grouse flushed straight away. My new 12-gauge side-by-side muzzleloader was easily mounted and followed the bird's flight through the open. A cloud of black powder smoke prevented me from seeing the charge of 1¼ ounces of mixed 8s and 9s connecting with the target, but I did see the crumpled grouse falling under the cloud of smoke.

I was greatly elated as Jinjer met the bird almost as it hit the ground—this was my first grouse taken with a muzzleloader! I couldn't have been more excited had it been a bull elk or moose. Of course, several minutes passed as I made over Jinjer with the grouse in hand, but then I thought about how the bird initially appeared, and I just had to go back and investigate.

I had no difficulty finding the exact point of the flush. At that spot there was a hole in the ground, the opening of—you guessed it—a groundhog (Appalachian vernacular for woodchuck) den!

Chapter 12

Grouse in the Grape Tangles

Alder Run Jinjer with the muzzleloader grouse.

Briars, Bells, and Tail Feathers

Shooting Blindly

All of us, on occasion, have followed through as a grouse disappeared in foliage before touching off the shot, only to achieve a good hit culminated by hearing the bird's wings beating against the ground—or, having our dog return with a bird in its mouth. Satisfying? Most certainly! However, on two separate occasions I have brought down a grouse by (safely) shooting the gun out of frustrated desperation. I say "safely" because of the angle the gun was fired...assuring me that the charge would be well above another person or dog.

The first time this happened, wildlife manager John Hawse and I were hunting Landacre Hollow on the George Washington National Forest in an oak-hickory clear cut. The cut area was so open, I didn't expect to see a grouse, but Tinker pointed in the middle of this cutover area. There were a few scattered white pine trees that were left with limbs to the ground; otherwise the hardwood regeneration was low. The bird Tinker was pointing left the ground almost at the precise moment the dog locked up, and quickly disappeared behind the pines. I fired a single shot, from the hip, in the direction of one of these pines, just to let Tinker know that I was trying. Tinker immediately ran out in the direction the grouse had traveled and—much to my amazement—I heard wings beating the ground followed by Tinker coming toward me with a bird in her mouth.

Howard Jones and I were checking out a new cover in western Randolph County, West Virginia. The few birds we found were flushing wildly ahead of my setters, Lance and Jennie, who knew what was going on and worked cautiously. But the birds still flushed wildly; we could hear but not see them. Again, out of desperation and wanting the dogs to know that we were paying attention, I shouldered my gun and fired blindly, but at a safe angle, in the general direction of the flush. I couldn't have been more surprised when Lance returned to me holding a grouse in his mouth.

Again, I wish to assure the reader that I am not advocating "sound shooting!"

The Hunt at Camp Mistake

Traveling north along West Virginia State Route 18, we came to the Doddridge/Tyler County line and soon found an unmarked, but prominent hollow on our map by the name of Camp Mistake. George Hanson and I were hunting with my young setter, Jeb. I had my doubts about hunting this area with the strange name—thinking this whole day might just be a big mistake! After all, this was November, 1959, and I was just as green at grouse hunting as my young setter that had been trained on wild quail and woodcock. But Jeb had been doing a great job and I was eager to see what he could do on grouse.

George had known something about the Camp Mistake Hollow and the grouse we were seeking, but this place was all new to me. It was soon apparent that the entire drainage had been sparsely occupied and farmed at some point in time but now the access road was a muddy lane that was all but obliterated by undergrowth. To me this was indeed pioneering at its best!

We had not worked our way up this drainage very far before we were into grouse, the numbers of which I failed to record in my journal. I doubt that I even thought about numbers that day. There was so much excitement: two young hunters with a young setter that was doing better than either of us ever anticipated.

I do know that Jeb was handling birds well for his age, and between us we had somehow knocked down and Jeb retrieved a total of three grouse! This was my first hunt with multiple grouse kills over my first English setter, 1½ years old.

On our way up this hollow, we went by an old unoccupied farmhouse and outbuildings and noticed that the doors were wide open. We decided to investigate the matter more closely on our way back down the hollow. Entering the house through open doors, we found the place completely furnished. It looked as if the folks who lived here simply walked away, leaving everything behind. The vintage items were especially interesting to me because my wife Ellie and I had recently begun furnishing our home with antiques. We noticed all sorts of oil lamps, stoneware, old chairs and the most interesting spinning wheel, apparently locally crafted based on the design and wood used in its making. This, I later found out, was a great wheel in complete and useable condition.

I left Camp Mistake Hollow thinking this was truly a red letter day—finding out that I really had a grouse dog along with the contentment of a fine day afield with a good partner and the intrigue of finding a furnished home from the past.

After inquiring around West Union as to the owner of the place on Camp Mistake, I finally found him, told him of our grouse hunt and finding the abandoned house. I asked him what was to become of the house furnishings. I was told that he did not consider any of the contents to be of value and that I had permission to take anything I could carry out of that hollow!

Ellie and I had to bide our time and wait for dry conditions to get a vehicle in and out of that place without having trouble. This grouse hunt was to be remembered in many ways, and every time I look at one of the items taken from the house, the name Camp Mistake comes to mind.

The Flask

In the past, I carried a flask of blackberry brandy in my vehicle. It is interesting to reflect on the number of times this flask actually came in handy and I was glad to have it aboard. The

George Hanson, Old Hemlock Jeb and Walt following the grouse hunt on Camp Mistake.
Photo by Ellie Lesser.

flask was always popular when I was part of a group of West Virginia biologists who hunted deer in Pennsylvania each year. It became a matter of tradition. Whenever one of the members of this party killed a deer, the flask was passed around in honor of the "trophy" and the person who filled his license. We even toasted the deer that had eluded us. The flask was especially welcomed—after the hunt—in cold, snowy weather!

There was one occasion when the flask really came in handy. Walt Saling and I were grouse hunting in Lewis County, West Virginia, in an abandoned hollow that had been strip-mined long ago, before complete reclamation of the sites was required. Spoil banks below the strip had been planted to food-producing shrubs like autumn olive and Tartarian honeysuckle, affording excellent habitat for grouse—while the benches aided access. It was a great piece of grouse cover.

We found the usual good number of grouse and did our share of both hitting and missing. An outstanding retrieve was the highlight of the hunt—for me, at least. Walt had hit a bird, pointed by both our dogs, which fell off the strip-mine bench and appeared to drop into an abyss and, of course, out of sight. My setter, Heather, marked the bird and took off into this deep, dark "hole in the ground." Heather was one of my better retrievers, but this was going to be a most demanding challenge. Naturally, we were ecstatic when Heather came up that steep slope with a mouth full of grouse. Walt gave a blessing that he didn't have to go down into that deep dark hole.

An hour before dark, we decided that we both had had enough for the day and dropped off the hill where our vehicle was parked, but missed it by several hundred yards. As we reached the bottom, we were confronted by a man dressed in a hooded, three-quarter length overcoat, and reeking of alcohol. He pretended to be caretaker of this property (I knew better) and accused us of poaching deer. It was obvious he knew nothing about grouse hunting. He had been finding dead deer with the hindquarters removed and thought he finally found the guilty party. As we stood talking with our double guns open with empty chambers, he told us that he was armed and not to try anything.

While I did not know him, I guessed he probably lived in a lone house at the mouth of this large hollow, that he lived alone and didn't have anything better to do than get drunk and act like the gamekeeper. Further, he did not understand our situation, so we had to be deer poachers! Walt had little experience with this type of individual, and was rightfully nervous about the matter.

We lured the "gamekeeper" to our vehicle on the pretense that he could see for himself; we had no deer or deer meat in our possession. The first thing I did, even before loading dogs, was reach under my seat and produced the flask. He accepted it with outstretched arms and eyes wide open. Now we were his long lost buddies and could do no wrong! He never did search the vehicle and acted like he could care less about deer once he had that flask in hand. And he wasn't armed!

Smokey

The Woodcock Boscage Benevolent Society (WBBS), a group of wildlife and hunting professionals, along with others interested in the welfare of the bird and its hunting, had their inaugural meeting in West Virginia. Wildlife Resources Division Chief T. R. "Pete" Samsell and his biologists hosted this initial meeting and participants stayed in cabins at Blackwater Falls State Park. The woodcock hunting was done in Canaan Valley and surrounding public lands.

The purpose of this gathering was to show the importance of Canaan Valley in respect to its unique vegetation (typical of more northern climes), flora, and fauna, and, of course its abundant woodcock numbers. Much of the 32,000 acres were privately owned and threatened by development of a large body of water and proposed pump storage electric generating project. The WBBS lasted a number of years and visited various states, in addition to a return to Canaan Valley.

Being familiar with the valley, I was assigned to guide WBBS participants on woodcock hunts. One member of my party was Charles Dickie, who at that time headed up the National Shooting Sports Foundation. Charley had a most beautiful full-masked tricolor English setter along with him, named Smokey. At that point in time, I thought Smokey was one of the best looking setters I had ever seen, because of his conformation and markings. I knew there were too many hunters for quality hunting in heavy cover, so we formed a line of men, some with a dog and some without, to work our first alder cover. Charley was on my right flank when I soon realized that Smokey was not with him. I asked where Smokey was and Charlie replied: "I left him in the car, Smokey does not hunt. His purpose in life is that of a photography model. We only use him for taking pictures."

A few woodcock were taken during this part of the hunt—certainly enough to put Smokey through the paces—and that is exactly what we did as soon as we returned to the vehicles. Charley told Smokey to sit and then placed a fresh woodcock in his mouth, which he readily took and proudly held head high. Someone then decided Smokey should hold two woodcock in his mouth at the same time, which Smokey happily obliged with a woodcock hanging out each side of his mouth. All the while, photographers were shooting Smokey holding "his" birds. A photographer/outdoor writer from the *Washington Post* was busy shooting photos. I heard this man call "profile Smokey" and was amazed to see Smokey promptly obey the command and present the photographer with a profile view.

Smokey was really putting on a show for the shutterbugs—but he was not without fault. We asked if Smokey would point. "You bet," was the answer, as Charley took a bird and placed it in front of Smokey. The setter took a couple steps toward the woodcock and stiffened into a stylish point. It was at this moment that Smokey's fault became very obvious—he had a most prominent erection! Apparently every time Smokey pointed, he displayed himself, forcing photographers to somehow hide the appendage or brush it out later in the darkroom.

Whose Dog Has The Best Nose?

It was one of those winters with too much snow to consider grouse hunting at the high elevations; even the moderately high slopes had too much snow for George Hanson and me to consider running our dogs. So we headed for an area east of the Allegheny Front in Grant County, where we pleasantly found snow-free ground to spend the day. We zeroed in on Monongahela National Forest clear cuts that were just on the downhill side of being good grouse habitat, but still held a few birds.

George was always a good friend, and fellow setter breeder. We worked very well together keeping the old Ryman bloodlines alive and well. Somehow, George always had a dog with the best nose of the bunch; this was according to his claim, of course. On the way over the mountains, there was much talk about the superior qualities of "Sport's" nose—one of his two setters along with us on that particular day. We had a lot of fun bantering back and forth about how great each of our dogs were, and of course, they being the very best setters anywhere! I always had a hard time topping George's stories, however.

We selected a timber haul road leading to a large clearcut for our initial hunt that day. Of course I was still hearing about Sport's wonderful nose attributes, as we hunted side by side on the old trail. As we reached a small grassy clearing, both Sport and my setter, Heather, started making game. Heather quartered upwind of the opening, entered the woods beyond, and soon locked up on point, flagged a bit, and moved on. Sport had left the scent also and moved ahead with George following. I looked around where Heather had pointed, as I usually do in search for some sign of a bird—when the unbelievable happened.

Right there on the ground was the remains of—guess what?—You got it! A Grouse! I couldn't believe what was before my eyes, after hearing what a great nose Heather's brace mate had—here laid, not a fresh kill, but the sun-dried partial carcass of a grouse! I picked up the grouse carcass and saw that, not 15 feet from where Heather had pointed, was just the sternum from a grouse carcass. Realizing that Heather had pointed something other than the grouse bone, I certainly could not resist taking full advantage of the situation and called to George to come on over and see proof of which dog has the best nose!

George Hanson with left to right: Tomboy's Dew Drop, Seneca Grouse Tinker, and Alder Run Heather after a day's hunt in the eastern panhandle of West Virginia.

Unusual Points of the Matter

Alder Run Heather pointing a woodcock while retrieving a woodcock.

In the life of a hunter when approaching a dog on point, there are times when the unexpected happens! The most common of the unusual points occurs when a single wild turkey holds tightly and the hunter is expecting a flush of a smaller bird. This has likely happened to most grouse hunters at one time or other.

On one occasion, I was exercising my young setter Tinker, on my own property, where she locked up tight in a stand of goldenrod. Making the most of the situation, I immediately went to her to encourage staunchness by stroking and applying pressure with my hand against her thighs. I had no idea what Tinker was pointing and my attention was riveted on her form. I suppose it was the humming noise that made me look ahead to see a very large swarm of honeybees attached to the goldenrod stems. Tinker was focused on the swarm just ahead of her nose!

There was the time we were hunting woodcock in Canaan Valley, shooting over my setter, Starr. Woodcock were abundant and Starr was handling the birds well. One of her points was remarkable, but all we could find was an entire family of raccoons taking refuge in the alders. Starr had to be led away, determined to tear into the 'coons. I learned that this otherwise calm and gentle setter hated furbearers and was determined to eliminate any critter covered with fur that might cross her path. And unfortunately, skunks were no exception!

The most spectacular "unusual" point occurred while winter grouse hunting with my male setter, Lance. We were working the slopes of Cheat Mountain, where a group of us lease a tract of land for hunting. Lance locked up solidly in a pile of downed treetops along an old log trail. I prepared myself for a grouse as I approached Lance, but there was no flush! It was unlike Lance to point rabbits, but he hadn't found anything in a while, so I thought he had a rabbit in that pile of brush.

I climbed up on a heavy log on the pile, and then jumped up and down; kicking the brush in an attempt to flush whatever was in the pile. At some point, I heard a faint noise that sounded like small trees rubbing against each other in the wind. I don't hear well, so I stopped moving to listen and took notice that it was perfectly calm—absolutely no air movement. It couldn't have been trees swaying in the breeze. Then I heard the sound again, and looking down between my feet, caught the movement of black fur. It was the sound of whining bear cubs! Very quietly, and carefully, I backed off the brush pile, patted Lance—who had been staunchly on point the whole time, and led him away. Lance found and pointed a grouse not very far from the bear den.

I reported Lance's bear den to local DNR biologists, and led them to the site a few weeks later. They drugged the sow, collected data, and installed a radio tracking collar on her. The two tiny cubs, born only weeks before, were left untouched inside the den cavity. My son brought along a couple teenagers to observe the process and be photographed with the drugged bear.

Epilogue

As a grouse hunter, I have gained a considerable amount of pleasure—and a way of life—for over 50 years. Following my setters through grape-tangled coves, thick shrub swamps, and even rock-strewn ridge tops has brought much delight and satisfaction. With Lisa Weisse, I have strived to answer questions that have been raised about the Ryman Kennels and the kind of setters George Ryman produced. Perhaps this work will inspire others to maintain the gun dog standards of George Ryman

When I started breeding setters with Burnell Davis and Bud Evans, the long range goal was not "to build a better mousetrap" but rather to maintain the bloodlines that George Ryman had developed for the purpose he developed them. This goal became increasingly important as time went on due to what we saw as the transformation of these setters by breeders other than George Ryman. We were not trying to breed a better setter to hunt grouse and woodcock, but in retrospect we probably were doing so. I learned early on to "only breed the best of the best," as Burnell had instructed us to do. In the long run I did see some improvement in our setter's ability in the grouse woods—surprising as this may seem, given that the later setters were encountering fewer grouse in their life spans than the earlier ones. Not surprising however, was the wonderful head conformation and close-coupled athletic bodies of these early setters that later proved to be exactly the setter type that George Ryman insisted his to be.

The grouse hunter of today faces great challenges. Foremost of those challenges, perhaps will be the sparse number of birds likely to be encountered in the Appalachian covers. This can affect our ability to produce quality grouse dogs. We can train our dogs on woodcock in these mountains but in the end it takes grouse to make grouse dogs. To have a fine day afield the modern hunter may need a different attitude than the hunter of yesteryear. The mindset of an experienced, veteran hunter should insure that the size of the game bag is less important than the enjoyment received just by being in the covers with the bird we cherish. There is so much to savor besides the weight and feel of a bird in the bag of a hunting coat. The dog's work is just one of those things that should be the main focus of a day afield.

Another challenge is the serious decline of grouse habitat. To understand the scope of the problem, all one has to do is examine the condition of our forests in winter or early spring—before leaf-out. At this time of year, the lack of grouse cover is starkly revealed. This is a result of our long overly-protected Appalachian forests.

It is useful to reflect on what these forests looked like prior to European settlement. There is a romantic tendency to visualize the original forest as being unbroken, a virgin forest with few openings and many large trees. Historical records of our forests reveal that they were never unbroken. Prior to European settlement, Native Americans cleared the land, setting fire to the woods regularly to maintain openings for various reasons. Fire, intentional or not, encouraged vegetation diversity suiting the needs of birds and mammals that require a young forest to survive. The ruffed grouse is a classic example.

The Ryman setter handles very well in the tight grouse and woodcock covers of the east but does every bit as well in other cover types, such as the prairie of southeast Idaho where this sage grouse was taken.

Epilogue

October Alder Run Dolly at home in an Appalachian covert.

Large mammals, like woodland bison and elk, were also once common in the eastern woodlands. The travels of bison maintained open areas that benefited other animals and birds needing young vegetation. Elk kept open the corridors by grazing on the abundant grasses and forbs resulting from the lack of forest canopy. The same grassy openings were used by birds as feeding areas, and young woody vegetation offered much needed nesting, resting and escape cover.

The exclusion of fire and large mammals, and, in some cases, the absence of recent logging, has given us a false impression of how the original forest appeared. As a result, our public lands in particular have matured (aged) and grown out of the habitat needed by many wildlife species dependent on young age forests—also referred to as early successional vegetation. Ruffed grouse and woodcock are two of at least 80 species that depend, at least in part, on this stage of forest development.

Our Appalachian forests have matured beyond the stage where they are capable of benefiting many wildlife species needing young vegetation in order to survive. Even in managed forests, young vegetation as found in clearcuts (where total forest canopy is removed) may be limited in number or size and thereby fail to provide the needs of these wildlife species. This is fragmentation of habitat for early successional species—like grouse and woodcock.

Public land agencies are under pressure from groups wanting to set aside large areas with no management, other than protection. This pressure sometimes results in congressionally designated wilderness areas—where no vegetation management, by law, can occur. Still another approach of the anti-management groups is that of litigation—taking agencies to court in efforts to stop any vegetation manipulation in the forest.

Another challenge to the grouse and woodcock hunter results from the lack of interest and understanding of hunting on the part of professionals assigned to the management of our public lands. I rarely find a hunter on the staff of any public agency (U.S. Forest Service or Fish and Wildlife Service) today. In my career days, one of the first questions asked at an interview for a wildlife management position—professional or non-professional level was "do you hunt or fish"? We rarely hired an applicant who did not participate in these outdoor activities.

Lately, I find that resource agencies and organizations are having difficulties finding qualified applicants for resource management positions. Students interested in an outdoor career now are more likely to pursue recreation activities other than hunting and fishing.

Grouse hunters generally tend to be loners and withdrawn from the masses. On the other hand, the opponents are well organized and funded. It is necessary that hunters join together and support organizations sharing our mutual interests. The Ruffed Grouse Society (RGS) is one such organization. RGS biologists interact with state and Federal agencies to promote habitat development and management. Other organizations include The Nature Conservancy, which acquires special lands, usually converted to state or Federal ownership and made accessible to sportsmen and other outdoor recreationists.

The Wildlife Management Institute, along with its partners, has joined together in a woodcock initiative to create thousands of acres of young forest that will be a big help to woodcock and other wildlife. This program consists of three regional initiatives addressing habitat in the Northern Forest, Appalachian Mountains, and Upper Great Lakes. You can find up-to-date contact information and learn about habitat demonstration areas in your region at www.timberdoodle.org.

Finally, interested individuals must get involved and make their voices heard. I am suggesting that such people get on land management agency mailing lists for proposed projects and let the agency know what you want or how you feel about the project. Insist that they address habitat management for the many critical early successional species. Keep in mind that in some cases, like national wildlife refuges, hunters footed the bill for the acquisition of these lands. Hunters are also paying for the management of state and Federal lands by purchasing licenses, due to Federal monies being reimbursed to the states for fish and wildlife restoration.

Stay involved with issues that will insure future generations the opportunity to experience sights and sounds of the ruffed grouse—a noble symbol of the wild!

Ryman Kennel Literature Examples

Grouse Hunter Davis:
Sir. Davidson & I went to Pa. and got two pups. Dave got a 4 months old pup. and I got a 6½ months old one. Both are Orange ticked
Mrs Vandine is in Florida for 2 or 3 weeks. Come over when you can

THE RYMAN SETTER

no charge to look.

As Ever
Tom Vandine

I took some movies at the Kennels.

NO BETTER SETTERS BRED

Bred Here at the Kennels continuously since 1916.

Bred selectively from Hunting Sires and Dams only.

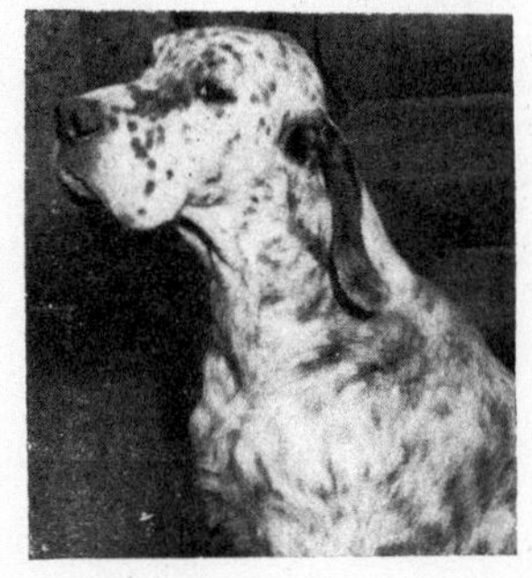

HANDSOME ENOUGH TO SHOW

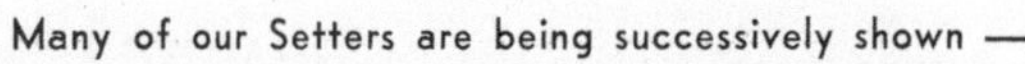

Many of our Setters are being successively shown —

yet are outstanding personal gun dogs with exceptional bird sense. Close working, natural pointing, biddable, easy to train, easy to handle and sensible. They are NOT wild field trial stock.

MOST OF
OUR
SETTERS
RETRIEVE
NATURALLY.

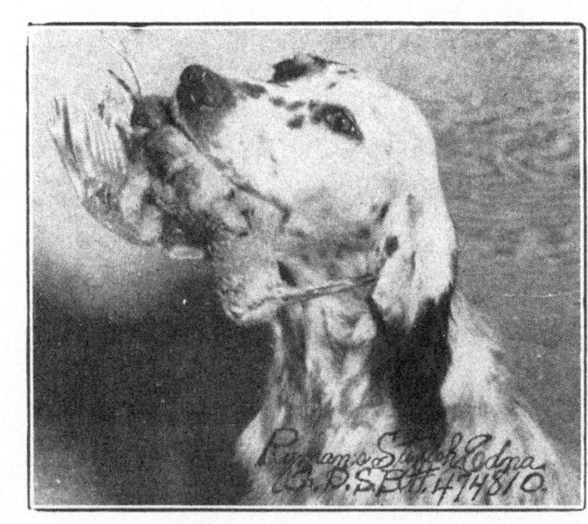

The end result of fifty years of selective breeding. The only continuously successful dual type Setter in existence today. The perfect gentlemen's shooting dog for grouse and wood cock.

Our puppies, either sex, blue or orange belton, are priced from $150.00 and up. Deposits and reservations accepted.

Our started Setters, either sex, blue or orange belton as available are priced from $250.00 and up.

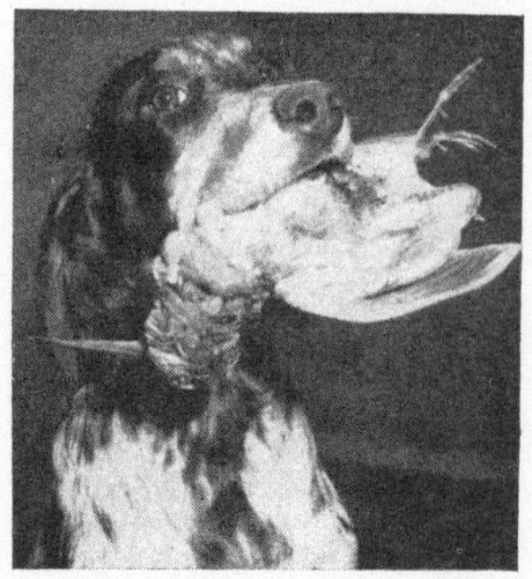

Our finished Setters, when available for purchase, are priced from $550.00 and up.

All of our Setters are offered subject to prior sale, are priced F.O.B. Our Kennels, are sold fully vaccinated, with a seven generation certified Pedigree and all papers necessary for registration in the F.D.S.B.

Mailing Address: Shohola, R.D., Pa.

RYMAN'S GUN DOG KENNELS
Shohola Falls,
Pike County, Pa.

Phone: Area Code 717-296-7631

RYMAN'S GUN DOG KENNELS
GEORGE H. RYMAN
OWNER, BREEDER, TRAINER, IMPORTER OF HIGH CLASS ENGLISH SETTERS
SHOHOLA FALLS, PIKE CO., PENNA.
Mr. H. B. Davis
Pennsboro, W. Va.
SHOHOLA
OCT
12
A.M.
1949
PA.
UNITED STATES POSTAGE
3 CENTS 3
UNITED STATES POSTAGE
3 CENTS 3

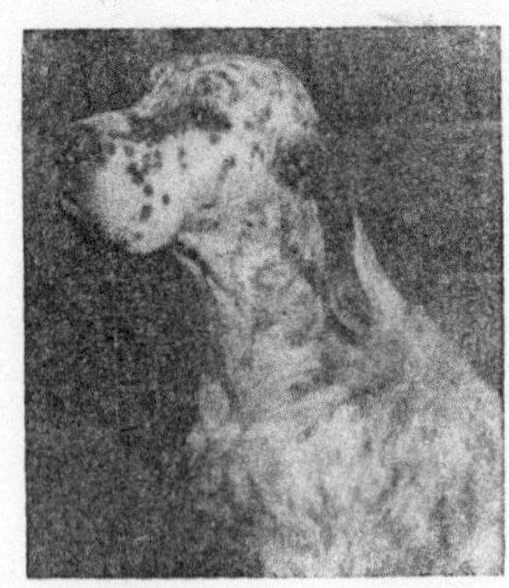

RYMAN'S GUN DOG KENNELS

GEO. H. RYMAN, Owner, Breeder, Trainer and Importer

SHOHOLA FALLS, Pike County, Pennsylvania, U. S. A.

1951
November 1st.

Dear Davis:

Your letter received the female Pup is a beautiful Pup. orange belton. has been wormed. twice has been given 10cc Pittman Moore Prevention Serum 2 weeks ago. yesterday gave the Pup its first Vaccination 5cc Virogen November 16 it should have 5cc Virogen and December 16th 5cc Virogen I listed them all and sold them all. but the Orange bitch for you. Prices quoted very less Vaccination She 10cc Serum no charge but the 5cc Virogen cost me $3 I could not hold young dogs here and run risk so started treating her. her Price Crated shipped all certified Papers $85.00
3.00 Virogen
$88.00
have lots of orders but no Pups. soon as we hear from you we will ship her. no Dogs shipped out of here later than Thursday each week as we Saturday express offices close. Thanking you I am

Geo H Ryman

Ancestors for several generations were field broken and heavily shot over from puppies up to their ripe old age. Blood most always proves its color. Trained and partly trained dogs and graded. Puppies, both sexes, for sale at all times. Visit Ryman's Gun Dog Kennels. Judge for yourself their type, color and field quality, obedience and work on game. Express office, Shohola, Pa.; Western Union office, Milford, Pa.; telephone, listed as Ryman's Gun Dog Kennels, is Milford 5361 Kennels are located on U. S. Route 6, twelve miles from Milford, Pa., and fifteen miles from Hawley, Pa.

THE FOUR SUPREME SISTERS

RYMAN'S GUN DOG KENNELS

SHOHOLA FALLS (Pike County), PENNSYLVANIA
Mailing Address: Shohola, R.D., Pennsylvania 18458
(Established 1916)

Telephone: Milford, Pa., 296-7631
(Area Code 717)

OUR FIFTY-SIXTH YEAR

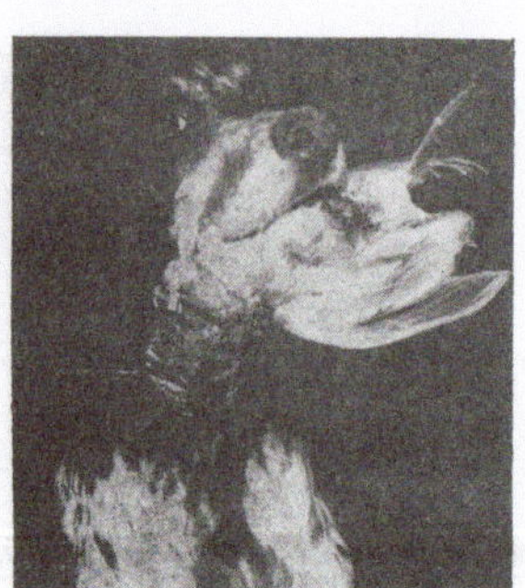

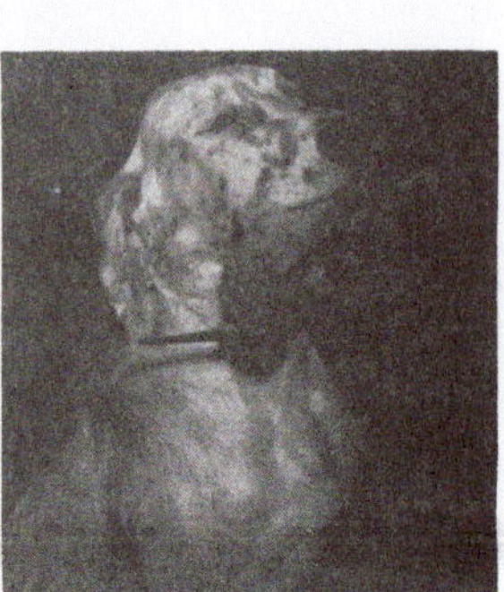

Photos of above Dogs are all Ryman bred setters fully trained on all four game birds.

WELCOME

TO

KATHY'S FARM

FISH & GAME CLUB

AND

RYMAN'S GUN DOG KENNELS

HUNTING LODGE: Located in old historic Greenbrier County nestled in West Virginia's Appalachian Mountains.

Club Office—Route 6, Box 27
Lewisburg, W. Va. 24901—Phone: 497-2090 or 497-2008

Chapter 3: George Ryman's Legacy

1. *Forest and Stream,* January 1917, "Grouse Dogs and Trials, Efforts to Establish Standards For a Gentleman's Shooting Dog," James Sansom.
2. Photos and pedigrees of Rummey Stagboro and Lakelands Nymph, along with other Laveracks, can be seen in Davis H .Tuck's *The Complete English Setter,* 1951 edition.
3. "Ryman's Gun Dog Kennels and Game Farm, G.H. Ryman, Proprietor, Shohola Falls, Pike County, Pennsylvania," 8 pages, illustrated, 1952.
4. Evans, George Bird, *Introduces—Men who have enriched our gunning through their bird dogs and paintings and experiences,* "Part I, George Ryman's Setters, Old Hemlock," 1990.
5. "Ryman's Gun Dog Kennels, G.H. Ryman, Proprietor, Setter Sale," early fall, 1954, 6 pages, illustrated.

Chapter 5: Laverick & Llewellin

1. *Pointers & Setters;* Derry Argue, Swan Hill Press, Shrewsbury SY3 9EB, England, 1993.
2. *The Setter, with Notices of the Most Eminent Breeds Now Extant; Instructions How to Breed, Rear, and Break; Dog Shows, Field trials, General Management, Etc.*; Edward Laverack, Broughall Cottage, Whitechurch, Shropshire. 1872.
3. *British Dogs, Their Points, Selection, And Show Preparation,* Third Edition; W. D. Drury, L. U. Gill, London; Charles Scribner's Sons, New York, 1903.
4. *The American Hunting Dog, Modern Strains of Bird Dogs and Hounds, and Their Training;* Warren H. Miller, George H. Doran Company, New York, 1919.
5. *The Kennel Club Stud Book: A Record of Dog Shows and Field Trials;* edited and compiled by Frank C. S. Pearce, published for the Kennel Club at the Field Office, London, 1874.
6. *The Sporting Dog,* by Joseph A. Graham, The MacMillan Company, New York, 1904.
7. This charge came mainly from people who were arguing against the movement to classify all dogs descended from Duke, Kate, Rhoebe, and the Laveracks as a separate breed. Notable among the early critics was Dr. Nicholas Rowe, the first owner of *American Field* magazine, who wrote in 1884 that "the cross was made, and its excellence proven before he owned any of them." Hochwalt and others have written similarly since. Although the qualities of Duke, Rhoebe, and their offspring were known, and Thomas Statter was the first person to breed a Duke x Rhoebe to a Laverack, there is little in the records that supports this assertion. When Llewellin's first Duke x Rhoebe-Laverack litter was born in May of 1872 the progeny of Statter's first were barely old enough to begin competing and none had even been entered in a trial yet.

Chapter 6: Roots of Rymans

1. *The Outing Magazine*, Vol. 27, February 1896, Outing Publishing Company.
2. *The Outing Magazine*, Vol. 37, March 1901, Outing Publishing Company.
3. *The Outing Magazine*, Vol. 58, July 1911, Outing Publishing Company.
4. *The Outing Magazine*, Vol. 50, July 1907, Outing Publishing Company.
5. It has been written that Beck bought Sir Roger de Coverly from Mangan as an adult,

reportedly as late as 1913. The registration, published in the *1908 American Kennel Club Stud-Book*, lists Beck as the owner.

6. Points were awarded for first place wins in the Open Class only. Shows of the era had numerous exhibition classes separate from the competition for points, and individuals or organizations frequently donated special trophies and prizes to promote certain types of dogs. For instance, at a 1911 show in Devon, PA Sir Roger de Coverly placed second in the "English Setter Club of America Championship Class for Dogs or Bitches that have won a club certificate or been placed at a public field trial."
7. An example is the 1909 Anthracite Kennel Club's annual show, where Sir Roger de Coverly placed first as the only dog entered in the Field Trial Class and third in the Open Class with five dogs entered.
8. This is not Sir Roger de Coverly's complete trial record, as previous to these two wins he was shown in a Field Trial Class. Field trial placements during that time are difficult to confirm. Although the AKC and numerous clubs sponsored trials, American Field is the only national organization that kept records from this period.
9. A.K.A. Blue Girl Janie in American Field records. We use the AKC spelling of Jaine, as this is the spelling used in the Ryman pedigrees.

Chapter 7: A Calendar of Ryman Setter Breeding

1. Sir Roger de Coverly II was born in 1911 but not registered until 1915. Ryman often delayed registration of his dogs for a few years, possibly to prove them first.
2. Sir Roger de Coverly did sire one litter out of a Ryman female, bred by Earl Lee of Starrucca, PA in 1916. Ryman sold this female to Lee in 1915 and he was the registered owner of two dogs from the litter (neither of which appear in any later pedigrees), so it's possible he was involved with this breeding in some way.
3. This dog was not an actual Mallwyd. It is common to find dogs that were registered using famous names they had nothing to do with.

Chapter 11: Hunting the Salad Bowls

1. A reference to grouse food habits can be found in the report *Ruffed Grouse Ecology and Management In The Appalachian Region...Final Report of the Appalachian Grouse Research Project, August 2004.* One of the largest ruffed grouse projects ever initiated was done to investigate the decline of grouse in the Appalachian region. This pioneering research effort was a six-year study encompassing state natural resources agencies in Kentucky, Maryland, North Carolina, Ohio, Pennsylvania, Rhode Island, Virginia and West Virginia and included various educational institutions. It provided new information concerning various aspects of grouse ecology and management in the Appalachian region. Data were collected from September 1996 through October 2002, on 3,118 grouse captures on 12 study sites. Copies of this report can be obtained from any of the state agencies involved in the study. Serious grouse hunters would do well to look it over.

Long, R., J.W. Edwards, R.L. Kirkpatrick, and A. Proctor. "Food Habits and Nutrition." *Ecology and Management of Appalachian Ruffed Grouse,* D. F. Stauffer, J.W. Edwards, W.M. Giuliano and G.W. Norman, editors, pp. 70-80. Blaine, Washington: Hancock House, 2011.

Barber, H.L., F. J. Brenner, R. Kirkpatrick, F.A. Servello, D.F.Stauffer, and F.R. Thompson. "Food." *The Wildlife Series: Ruffed Grouse.* S. Atwater and J. Schnell, editors, pp. 268-282. Harrisonburg, Pennsylvania: Stackpole Books, 1989.

THE REAL
RYMAN
SETTER